HONORABLE INTENTIONS

CHERYL MERSER

HONORABLE   INTENTIONS

The Manners of Courtship
in the '80s

New York **ATHENEUM** 1983

Library of Congress Cataloging in Publication Data

Merser, Cheryl.
    Honorable intentions.

    Bibliography: p.
    Includes index.
    1. Courtship. 2. Dating (Social customs)
3. Love. 4. Etiquette. I. Title.
HQ801.M54   1983   646.7'7   82-45180
ISBN 0-689-11311-0

For my mother and my father,
and for Richard King

My "passion" dated from that day. I think, looking back, that my feelings then were like those that a man must have when he embarks on his career: I had already ceased to be merely a young boy; I was a lover. I have said that my passion dated from that day; I might add that my suffering began with that same day.

Ivan S. Turgenev, *First Love*

Acknowledgments

I AM GRATEFUL to the many people, too numerous to name, who gave me encouragement all along, and to countless others who listened politely for years I rattled on about courtship. Specifically, for help in one way or another, I'd like to thank Sara Binder, Claudia Stern, Cindy Mullaney, Burk Uzzle, Bob Loomis, Amanda Urban, Mary Vespa, Gary Fisketjon, Melanie Fleishman, Jill Bernstein, Caroline Little, Susan Horton, Carol Schneider, Milly Marmur, Joe Fox, Pat Eisemann, Anne Freedgood, Susan Richman, Harry Ford, Elaine Markson and Geri Thoma. I'd like to thank, too, all the people who took the time to fill in questionnaires, or to be interviewed in person. I'm especially grateful to Judy Kern, my editor at Atheneum. And most of all, I'd like to thank Jason Epstein, Erroll McDonald and Carolyn Reidy.

Preface

RECENTLY I ran across one of those nine-out-of-ten surveys claiming that nine out of every ten Americans believe that love is the most important ingredient for happiness. Aside from wondering idly whether the same ten Americans are questioned for all these surveys, and who these ten people might have been, I wouldn't for a moment doubt the results of this particular survey.

Oddly, for a culture as obsessed with love as ours is, there is pathetically little around that gets to the heart of the subject. You can find out all you want to know about sex; about singles' lives and meat-rack singles' bars; about sex; about marriage, divorce and remarriage; still more about sex; about how loneliness affects our health and life spans—and even more about sex. Fine. But there's another round of questions that increasingly concern many of us and which, thankfully, neither clinical nor social scientists have bothered to touch: What are the rituals by which we learn to express love, the "rules" that used to be known as the etiquette of courtship? More simply, what we don't know anymore is how to get from Point A in courtship to Point B, what the stages of courtship are and what to expect as a love affair turns into what we so prosaically call a "relationship."

I suppose that you become "single" once you're old enough to have stopped having chaste infatuations and started up with sex. Or when you've ended a marriage or a long, serious affair. Or when the only category that applies is "available." For me, the initiation into single-dom was a painful one. Shortly after I graduated from college I began living with a man who, a couple of years later, left me for someone else. Apart from my all-around misery at my circumstances there was the dread I felt knowing that sooner or later I would have to venture out into the social world again, that I hadn't the first clue about how grownups these days went about dating and that I'd never in a million years qualify for a convent, even if I had wanted to enter one. The thought of going out with someone new, and the thought of starting another sexual relationship, made me feel—although I had dated for years—utterly bewildered.

I thought of various unattached friends of both sexes—the trouble they seemed to have meeting nice people; negotiating when to have sex, and why; assessing where affairs were leading. I also thought of my mother, twenty-some years my senior, and others like her, recently divorced and now puzzling over the same questions that plagued my friends and me. (To keep the record straight, my mother has since remarried, happily.) From what I could see at that point, dating took a considerable emotional toll on men as well as women and no matter what age. The whirlwind singles' world I kept reading about didn't seem to exist in real life, and even if it did I was certain it wasn't for me. And from just a quick look around, it didn't appear that the questions I had would resolve themselves even with time and experience—many of my friends had been bouncing around from unhappy relationship to unhappy relationship for years.

At the same time, I was amazed to find that, even in my enormous unhappiness and as reluctant as I was to risk being hurt so badly again, thoughts of falling in love began to work their way back into my daydreams, like images of chocolate sundaes into a dieter's. If you consider love a requisite for happiness, as those nine out of ten Americans presumably do, you're hooked.

The questions that concerned me most, once I did begin going out again, had to do with the *process*: I couldn't remember—or, more accurately, had never learned—how to behave in grown-up dating situations. Should I offer to pay? insist on it? Was I expected to sleep with so-and-so on the first date, the second, the third? What would he think if I did sleep with him? if I didn't? What if he seemed to expect breakfast and I didn't have any muffins? What if he didn't call back? Could I call a man and tell him I have, just happen to have, a pair of theater tickets? How would I know if I was in a relationship or not? And so on. The very questions I found myself discussing endlessly with friends, and find myself discussing still.

At any rate, it hit me at some point that an understanding of courtship and how it works is fundamental to understanding love and even sex—and this in a time when no one has any idea what the new "rules" for all these things are or how to apply them, when we're all, as it were, "coming from different places."

It's at the expense of attention to the details of courtship that we have so glorified sex. There's something really wrong when you can easily find a book on the bestseller list called *How to Make Love to a Man* (or a woman, or to each other) or *Nice Girls Do* yet nothing on the kindest ways to end a love affair, how to say no if you really mean sometime or what someone means, *really* means, when he or she claims to need "space." Not all questions about courtship, love or sex can be answered by books, of course, but to talk about sex and love without first giving some thought to courtship is something like learning open-heart surgery before you know enough anatomy to tell a vein from an artery.

At the risk of sounding like a crabby Puritan, what we really need, and what I hope this book will provide, is a presentation of the customs we adults practice for meeting, dating, sleeping together and falling in love—so that at least we all have the same idea of what to ask of and expect from one another while searching for happiness in love.

It's no coincidence that our thoughts about love have changed along with our ideas about how a proper courtship is conducted. In your grandmother's day, nobody much beyond the age of eighteen or nineteen would spend much time reading about the personal pursuit of love. Well before Grandma hit the age of twenty, she knew that it was more important for her to find a husband than it was for her even to learn to read. First things first. The first thing for kids now is deciding what color their parachute is, or finding a way to get on in the world. By the time we get around to thinking about love in a serious way, poof, we're all grown up. We're different now from what Grandma and her friends were like, and we expect other things than they did from love, from sex and even from courtship. And the courtship etiquette we've chosen reflects both the way we think about love and our new attitudes toward and ideas about sex.

I have chosen purposefully to use the words "courtship" and "etiquette" throughout this book, not to be deliberately archaic or sentimental but because these are the words that define precisely what I'm talking about. Etiquette is a French word for "ticket," not the *billet* kind you remember from French 101—that's a ticket to get you into a movie or onto a plane—but a card of identity like a passport, a signal among people who speak the same language. Etiquette is not a set of rules to separate ill-mannered goats from polite sheep, but rather a code meant to draw people together. Nor is it something practiced by other generations but not by us; it's waiting in line at the bank, sending back those irritating (and easy to lose before you remember to) little wedding R.S.V.P. cards, shaking hands, saying good morning to the nastiest person in your office. And etiquette isn't arbitrary fascism; usually there are perfectly sensible reasons behind the rules of good manners.

The word courtship comes from "court"; the best manners, those to be emulated by the population at large, were those established at court. This is not to advise you to imitate the manners practiced at the White House—you might end up with a lot of nice china but not too many friends if you do—but to point out that matters of courtship and of love call for the most decent behavior we can manage. I'd much rather get caught using the soup spoon for my salad than be needlessly unkind to someone I care about.

The word "manners" comes up a lot, too, and here I've taken a few liberties. You can use manners as in good or bad manners, or to describe the way a group of people behave—a comedy of manners, for example. But I think you can also apply the idea of manners to emotional concerns—what if you would never think to wear white to a wedding but wouldn't think twice if your child were rude to someone you loved? When it comes to courtship, the subtler manners your feelings cause you to display are more important than the *pro forma* "do this, don't do that" kind of manners that are little more than rules to memorize.

Early in the writing of this book, I explained to an acquaintance that it was about the etiquette of courtship. "Ah, a sex book," he said, but then slowly and patiently, as if he were talking to someone from the moon, he went on, "but there are no rules anymore."

The "rules" here, though, are those that will help us define and understand and get through what I've discovered are distinct stages of courtship, beginning with the first meeting and ending with an impasse at which you must decide to stay together in one of the conventional ways or to part and seek your futures separately.

There's a first-time sexual etiquette, for example, to enable you to make each other feel more comfortable. There's a new way to involve friends, family and children in a romance, to offer a bureau drawer to a frequent lover, to work out financial arrangements, to confront impotence, to say yes, no or possibly some other time. There are ways to understand what your lover wants from your relationship, and there are ways to get the thing off to a good strong start.

The etiquette of courtship is not an etiquette to learn by rote (Miss Dishwater regrets that she cannot attend your party...), but a code with a good deal of leeway that, despite its inevitable personal variations and unexpected turns, includes among its rituals bits and pieces of behavior from the days of Adam and Eve as well as manners from, God help us, the *Love Boat*. And if this book can do one thing, I hope it will prevent you from hurting others and from getting hurt yourself.

I am not a social scientist, but then courtship is not a science. To prepare for writing this book I have read as much about courtship and love as I could, and traced the changes reflected in etiquette and social-history books published over the years. In addition to my own (cleverly disguised) stories and those of my friends, I've relied on personal interviews and questionnaires—and shameless eavesdropping. The questionnaires were distributed to friends of friends of friends throughout the country, and the approximately three hundred returned were from men and women between the ages of nineteen and sixty-three, with annual incomes ranging from $7,000 to far more than I ever hope to make.

As I was putting together this research I began to see—with that exciting and nagging sense that one is on to something—that our manners truly have not come to us in a void, that we still rely in part on a centuries-old tradition that tells us how to love. Many of the customs we live by today are not, as we tend to describe them, "new" and "modern" and certainly not "revolutionary." Every age is distinguished by what it thinks of as its new, modern and even revolutionary customs, but on examination, every culture owes much to its history, which, for us, is full of some wonderfully romantic and practical stuff, and which helps explain how we got to where we are today.

For all its continuity, the etiquette of courtship also changes with the social conditions of the era; you can tell something about it by looking at the fashions, literature, politics and economics of the day. And for us, courtship draws in the ridiculous (sharing a toothbrush, say) along with the sublime (an evening of the most beautiful love-making that you'll remember long after you and your friend have turned to others).

One of our mistakes is that we talk about courtship the way the FDA talks about chickens. We don't love people; we have "love objects." "Significant," "meaning-ful," "commitment," "relationship," "pair-bonding," "motivation," "fulfillment"—the words we use are joyless, filled with the dead air of therapists' offices and too remote to have much to do with what happens between two people, both in and out of bed. Courtship might be all these things—but it's more. It's thinking about love together, and learning new things about sex each time.* It's about decency, giving and changing. Courtship, despite all the energy and hard work it requires, and all the aggravation, can even be fun. It's an art, one you can learn a lot about simply by practicing. And happily, courtship is a rare art—because even if you practice it a little off key, if you're sincere and enthusiastic about it, nobody's going to accuse you of being tone deaf.

---

*The discussion of sex, in case you feel the need to skip around, begins in Chapter Six.

Contents

HONORABLE INTENTIONS

Chapter One

Courtship:
Revisionist Thinking

IT WOULD be absurd to begin an honest discussion of contemporary courtship with the assumption that we're all going to live happily ever after; I know we won't, you know we won't, divorce lawyers know we won't. Yet the myth that we will persists beyond all logic or statistics, and despite ourselves we still somehow believe that court-ship is a "procedure" you shouldn't have to go through more than once—like geometry class—and that it has a beginning (the meaningful glance), a middle (fireworks) and a happily-ever-after ending.

The sad truth is that most of us spend our courting time muddling through broken hearts and recovering from broken marriages, chasing promising leads who ski off to Aspen to "find themselves" and yawning through a lot of excruciatingly dull dates in between.

We also have as a part of our myth a clear picture of courtship as a scene involving nubile, blushing youngsters, benches under apple trees and a Papa off in the distance oiling his shotgun—and not a scene, as is more likely the case today, involving aging baby-boom types in singles' bars, or middle-aged divorcés in leisure suits vacationing at Club Med.

If one thing is clear to us it's that the old rules no longer apply to new circumstances in a world where almost nothing is predictable or for certain. There appears to be no order in the social order. During the 1981 Christmas season, for example, when the presumably antiwar Vietnam generation had settled down to raising children, the toy industry reported a surge in, of all things, the sales of G.I. Joe dolls. As for the fashion industry that year, it couldn't decide between miniskirts and the prairie look. As we swore in a devoutly anti-abortion president, Americans set a new record for the number of abortions performed. Automobile companies lost billions, the unemployment rate soared—and *Vogue* announced a return to formal dinner parties. Never before had I received so many wedding announcements or, for that matter, heard more rumors of divorce among people I know. Perhaps the world has always been this contradictory; I doubt it.

But cultures have gone through upheavals before and people have always managed to adapt as the need arose. When it comes to something as important to us as courtship is, people have always been especially creative in adapting the rituals of mating to the prevailing social conditions—call it romantic Darwinism, call it survival.

In some European countries two or three hundred years ago, the custom of handfasting was part of the courtship ritual. A couple intending to marry lived together for a year and a day before a wedding was planned. If the woman became pregnant or gave birth during that time the wedding was announced; if not, the couple separated. The point is that Europe was expanding rapidly during those years; the need for children was, at the time, what marriage was all about. And the needs of the culture are always what determine its customs. Handfasting was by no means the first custom to sanction pre-marital sex or to regulate the supply of and demand for children by adjusting customs or morality. During the Middle Ages, when the mortality rate was very high, illegitimate children were commonplace and perfectly acceptable. The only restriction such children had to put up with was that they could marry only other illegitimate offspring (not a problem—there were plenty to choose from) and that they were barred from inheriting property or the throne. Thus the population flourished—and at the same time lineages were kept intact. Courtship adapted to the needs of the day.

The custom of bundling, which had its origins during the handfast years in Europe, crossed the Atlantic with the Puritans and found its way to Colonial New England. Bundling allowed a couple to court all night in bed— fully dressed, as propriety demanded, and within earshot of other members of the family. The custom provided an opportunity for courtship even though the cramped, cold houses of the humbler classes gave the courting couple no real chance for privacy, not to mention warmth, especially during standard late-evening courting hours. In addition, bundling was a comfortable and even restful way to settle down after having worked from dawn til dusk. Often, for extra moral protection, a bundling board was planted smack in the middle of the bed, and the custom was considered safe enough to allow the occasional weary stranger a bed in which to bundle down (up?) for a night with the daughter of the house.

Sermons and broadsides denouncing bundling kept a lot of people busy for years, but bundlers paid no attention until they could afford to add parlors to their homes. Once that happened and no one *had* to bundle anymore, the practice simply ceased.

Our own courtship customs are no less the result of practical necessity than bundling was for the Puritans. That the sexual revolution has changed the rituals of courtship is hardly news, but the sexual revolution didn't exactly come out of thin air. It, too, resulted from profound changes in society. Revolutions are started by people, not by Pills, and the biggest change in courtship in our lifetime is that adults of all ages are likely to be out courting—where in other, earlier times, grownups would be safely tucked away at home with their families. Adults have sex. So when adults are out courting it makes perfect sense that they'll sneak sex into the rituals of courtship. With courtship more or less for everyone, it's a whole new game, with a whole new set of rules.

In the past, even the recent past, full-fledged grownups who found themselves courting did so in a serious, grownup way, if also with some embarrassment—the Widower Perkins, clutching a bouquet of violets and a box of chocolates, walked down the lane to visit Miss Simmons, the spinster schoolteacher. Such better-late-than-never relationships were for the sake of matching up society's loose ends. After a few shy encounters, or so the story goes, the couple would marry quietly and take their expected places with the rest of society.

There was no clue, not even a footnote in the etiquette books, to warn us that we would by now have become a culture of some fifty million single loose ends, a society of unmated socks in a laundry basket as big as North America. But then we rarely anticipate such huge changes in the way we live (no one invented TV dinners, for example, until after someone else invented TV); even so, societies and the people who live in them have always managed to adjust as they go along.

Nevertheless, most of us still find the idea of courtship somehow embarrassing, something that conjures up high school proms and necking in the back seats of cars. And it doesn't make it any less embarrassing that everyone else you know is going through it, too. To begin with, the language of courtship—boy friend and girl friend—is the language of the young. How can you have a girl friend if you're no longer a boy? We make do by muttering about a current "friend" in the hope that proper emphasis on the word will express the intended meaning. We don't much like to "date"; instead we "go out" as if we were headed for the supermarket. And even when we become lovers we're wary: "Oh, yeah, I'm seeing this guy" is not, given the richness of the English language, the most eloquent way to state where matters stand between you and your lover.

It's natural that by the time you're old enough to have had more lovers than you do fingers to count them on, you are likely to feel diffident, if not downright cynical, about courtship. Picture, for example, the successful career woman on her millionth blind date and at a loss for the small talk she'll need to get through it, or untrained in the karate she might need to get home safely—and alone. Or the overwhelming shyness a newly divorced man of forty feels picking up the telephone to call a woman for a date for the first time since he was married seventeen years ago. If form follows function, the point of courtship as it originally evolved was to make it easy to zero in on one lifetime mate, or several, if you happened to be hardier than your spouse. These days, lifetime mates are about as plentiful as unicorns, and once you've played the dating game for a while it's impossible not to wonder when and how—or even whether—it's all going to end.

The English writer Ian McEwan has written a not very subtle short story called "First Love, Last Rites," in which the end of a young couple's first love affair coincides with the violent death of a pregnant rat. That's pretty shocking symbolism for what I would guess is McEwan's message: for these people there's nowhere to go but down after the innocent joys of first love. Yet most of us know, somehow, that we simply can't think about love that way. While it's true that with each passing love affair we lose something precious and irreplaceable, it's also true that, no matter how deeply we might grieve over a passing love, we are, in matters of the heart, indomitable. As recent studies of sexuality among the aging (to say nothing of simple observation) demonstrate, we endlessly seek out love, the affirmation of sex and someone to wake up next to in the morning. And this goes way beyond the Darwinian notion that we court in order to breed; the man and woman who marry at eighty have reasons of their own to be in love.

So it's time to stop thinking of courtship as nothing more than a necessary prelude to the happily-ever-after end; courtship nowadays is, at least for many of us, as inevitable as death and taxes—and we might as well set about making it more pleasant. As Emerson so gently describes the lifelong process, "It matters not whether we attempt to describe the passion at twenty, thirty or at eighty years. He who paints it at the first period will lose some of its later, he who paints it at the last, some of its earlier traits."

For adults, each new notch on the divorce tally heightens our apprehensiveness toward love. It's hard to trust your own feelings—or anyone else's—when according to some estimates about 60 percent of today's marriages end in divorce. If the same percentage of tax returns ended in audits, think how scrupulously you'd go over your income-tax return before you put it in the mail.

On the other hand, more divorces than not end in remarriage, a fact that shows pretty clearly that as a culture we still have a firm belief in the enduring possibilities of love—or what Dr. Johnson called the "triumph of hope over experience." For the first time in history, there are enough divorced people around to effect significant changes in the etiquette of courtship, but in fact the divorced people I've talked to are as confused about the new rules as those of us who have been single all along. Reflecting on the changes they've found in courtship since their divorces, many people compare the experience of "coming out" after a marriage has ended with how Rip Van Winkle must have felt after his twenty-year nap.

A woman I know, an attractive New York editor in her fifties, still laughs over her favorite "re-entry" story. She had been married for more than twenty years, and when she finally got her divorce the thing that frightened her most was what time and the sexual revolution had done to her ideas about courtship. Her first date went smoothly enough, more or less following the rituals her mother had handed on to her many years back. She relaxed and eagerly accepted a second invitation, for dinner at the man's elegant duplex apartment. "He had a house-boy," she recalls, "who served the most wonderful dinner. After the coffee, though, he turned to my date and asked, 'Will there be one for breakfast or two?' I couldn't believe it!" At that moment she came right out of her time warp.

Now that so many courting couples take sex in their relationships for granted, the dimensions and the possibilities of fledgling love have changed utterly. As we'll see, the etiquette of courtship is often inseparable from the etiquette of sex. Placing sex right out in the open and not hidden away changes the story from beginning to end. Think of sex as the glittering city of Oz, down at the far end of the Yellow Brick Road. What a different story it would be if Oz were at the beginning of the road instead—as sex is now in our courtship story.

When the vanguard of the sexual revolution, whoever they were, first sounded "Cut!" to everything about the Puritan ethic, they were onto something big. As soon as we heard the revolutionary cry, most of us, afraid to be left behind, grabbed a copy of *The Joy of Sex* and dove into the nearest waterbed long before we could possibly figure out what we expected or hoped to find under the covers.

Like other successful uprisings, the sexual revolution created its own bureaucracy, with special jobs for those people loyal to the cause. From the cover of *Time*, for example, Masters and Johnson, deadly earnest in their white lab coats, measured with various scientific gadgets the sexual excitement levels and response patterns of their "clients." In much the same way as the early Bolsheviks decided what the workers and peasants really wanted, Masters and Johnson and others like them have made clear decisions, without consulting us, about our sexuality.

The revolution in sexual awareness also spawned sex clinics all across the country to "cure" cases of sexual dysfunction which, before the revolution, we never knew existed. (More white lab coats, obviously the uniform of the revolution.) The Pleasure Chest, a New York–based emporium that sells, among other things, plastic penises, numerous kinds of vibrators and rubber suits, is now a multimillion-dollar business leasing franchises, like McDonald's, and charging as much for its mail-order catalog as Tiffany's does. Hundreds of women make money on the side by organizing parties where they display and sell the latest in erotic costumes and equipment. Sex is big business.

Although somehow or other the human species has always managed to hear enough about sex to keep itself going, these days we pass the word along as if we had invented sex education all by ourselves, and just in the nick of time. For beginning readers there are primers on sex, and even before these kids learn how to read at all, there are sex storybooks for their mommies and daddies to read to them at bedtime. By the time our kids reach puberty, they are saturated with sexual information. For most of us who believe in the revolution, all this seems new, improved, liberal.

The sexual revolution is clearly a success. Or is it? To me, despite all I've read, heard and thought and learned firsthand about sex, it's more a mystery than ever, a mystery I'm quite certain I wouldn't want to unravel entirely.

This is not to say that the sexual revolution shouldn't have happened or that it didn't live up to its promise. I'm grateful to those stalwart pioneers who risked their necks to make it possible for me to sleep with whom I choose. The point instead is that in our eagerness to consolidate the revolution we have probably made too much of sex—and at the same time too little. When you stop to think about it, all the sex hype that surrounds us hasn't done nearly so much for our lives as, well, the wheel did. But even a wheel by itself won't do you much good; you have to attach it to an axle and the axle to a cart and the cart to a horse before you get much out of it. In the same way, sex by itself, detached from a person you care about, might get one of you pregnant, but it won't make you happy.

During the interviews I did for this book, and during more late-night phone conversations with friends than I can begin to count, the question of courtship came up repeatedly: Why didn't Jack call when he said he would? Why does Carol always talk about her last boyfriend? If Sally loves me so much, then why does she want to see other people, too? For most of us, the details of sex— the newest position, the occasional premature ejaculation, the love-making session that lasted an hour and a half longer than usual—mean much less in the long run than what happens from day to day outside the bedroom.

On my questionnaires I asked the simple question, "What aspects of a relationship—companionship, shared goals, sense of humor and the like—would you place before sex?" The answers didn't surprise me. "Almost all. These things make good sex." "All belong on the same high level as sex." "Without these, sex can't mean anything." The agreement was virtually unanimous. The sexual revolution has given us the freedom to talk about sex as casually as we might about the weather, but this doesn't mean that we *think* about it casually. It makes perfect sense that we think and talk and worry about sex more than our forebears did; we have to make many more choices about sex than they did, and we have to reach complicated conclusions about it on our own. All their sex decisions were made for them by their culture; they had other things to worry about. But that doesn't mean that we're sex-obsessed, or any less interested than our ancestors in being principled about sex or without ideas about how we want to govern our behavior. Changing morality (and morality is always changing) is not the same as amorality.

It hasn't been easy working sex into our courtship etiquette, and we have made mistakes as a result: sleeping with the right person at the wrong time or the wrong person at the right time; using sex as a weapon or toy; becoming pregnant stupidly or carelessly. The revolution has taught us that sex can be easy. We have always known that love is not.

The sexual revolution did not happen in isolation, but was part of a larger movement, a movement that gave us freedom of many kinds to choose how we want to live. Society doesn't insist as strenuously as it did even in my parents' day that we marry and have children. The stigma attached to being single has to some extent disappeared (a "single woman" at least *sounds* different from a "spinster"), and two people have still another socially acceptable alternative to marriage—they can live together. We grownups, now that we've taken over courtship, have given the old story a multiple-choice ending, and sometimes we try out all the answers before we decide which one is right.

It's not by chance that history has chosen our recent past for such a vast social experiment. It has usually been true that in times of cultural stability, prosperity and confidence, morals and manners relax. The richer we are as a society the more freely we behave. Conversely, during times of cultural uncertainty, the moral code tightens up. When our survival seems threatened, we look for order and tradition to hold our lives together. (One of the tricks for measuring morality, according to Thorsten Veblen in *The Theory of the Leisure Class*, and others, is to figure out how a culture feels about girdles. When the women are so tightly bound they can hardly breathe, it usually means that the manners and morals of a culture don't allow for much breathing room, either.)

In the booming Twenties, the flappers set the moral tone, despite cries of rage from those leftover Victorians who still thought they controlled the moral barometer. By the time of the Depression years, only a decade later, we tightened the moral and sexual reins, squeezed ourselves into girdles and lengthened and narrowed skirts so that women could hardly move their legs, much less show their knees. Later, during the war, if an unmarried couple slept together before the man went off to the front, it was considered more an act of patriotism than simply a lark.

We were recovering, cautiously, in the Fifties. As if testing ourselves for injuries after a fall, we were testing our culture to see if this time it would hold together, and hoping, working, for a brighter future. We did our testing from inside what we thought was the safest institution of all: the nuclear family.

The Sixties were different. The cautious promise of the Fifties seemed to have become a reality, and we thought we were on top of the world. The baby-boom generation of the late Forties and Fifties, large enough to set its own rules and the first to come of age with the Pill, took over. Comfortable and assured of a shining future, it was easy for this generation to rebel against residual puritanism. It wasn't enough anymore to have a life; one had to have a "life-style." The impact of these new values continued throughout the Seventies. More women were college-educated, and more than half, by the end of the decade, were working and marrying later, or not at all. (Had they still been marrying earlier, there wouldn't have been much of a sexual revolution—no one would have had the time before settling down.) For the first time in history, children were considered a luxury and not a necessity, and for these women the decision to have them was easily postponed til the last minute. Those who did marry discovered that more often than not their marriages ended in divorce, and before they knew it they were out courting again. The only girdles these women knew about were jeans so tight you had to hold your breath to maneuver your way into them.

Now, in the Eighties, we are again confronted with a moral upheaval. The prosperity that a few years ago made us feel secure enough to experiment with new ways of living has crumbled under the weight of recession and inflation and the discovery that the "good times" we had enjoyed were going to cause the bad times we're having today. Everything is now in doubt. We're fighting to keep the jobs, security and life-style we have, but it's clear that the moral atmosphere is tightening up again.

In an article about the New York housing shortage, *New York* magazine observed a while back that the baby-boom generation currently is more absorbed by real estate than it is by sex. That may be funny, but it's more: If you're going to devote yourself to pleasure you first had better have a place to live. And if you're going to have sex and a hard-core designer life-style, you had better first have a job.

The anti-abortion right-to-lifers are out to change our morality, as are those who are trying to ban *Huckleberry Finn* from the libraries of our schools and other extremist groups. But with or without fanatics, the morals of a society, the morals of courtship, never stop changing of their own accord. A year or two ago, some of the women's magazines published articles about what they called the "New Chastity," which turned out to be not "chastity" at all but nothing more than a personal preference among men and women not to sleep together until they were good and ready to, and unless they really "felt something" for each other. Some people quoted in the articles actually admitted that they had been chaste for as long as six months. Apparently, for some people the pressure to have sex had gotten so far out of hand that they were doing the only sensible thing in retaliation: putting sex back where it belonged.

It's also interesting to note that a number of major

etiquette books have been published in the past couple of years, and more are being written now, after a virtual dearth of them in the Sixties and Seventies. Etiquette books pass on a culture's traditions intact; we didn't need traditions or etiquette books in the do-your-own-thing years. As for girdles, while we may not *call* them girdles, for the first time in years the stores are full of control-top thises and control-top thats.

The moral code and the courtship rules for our times are once again in flux. On the one hand, we're still confused by the sexual and moral freedom that has recently come our way; on the other, we're up against a time when free and easy living, reluctant as we are to lose it, may well be more than we can afford. Love, whose history pre-dates even the oldest person you've ever met, will survive and adapt. And if we too are to survive and adapt, so will sex.

The practice of courtship should adapt, too. But courtship is an art that can't be analyzed in the same way you can chart morality or the state of marriage at a given time or even sexual behavior. Unlike love, which always throws thinkers into a metaphysical tizzy (What is love? Is love virtuous or self-indulgent? Is love defined by the culture or is it characteristic of the human species?), courtship is an art we perfect as we practice it. And in these anti-rule, latter age-of-narcissism days, we've let courtship slip. My sense, which is reinforced by the people I've talked to since I began this book, is that if we think about it we can restore some of courtship's charm and meaning—if only to make the ritual clearer to all of us, so that we can get through it with a little less pain and confusion.

One thing that bothers me is that most of us are down on courtship. The very thought of a "date" is enough to send many of us running home to watch a *Gilligan's Island* rerun, which is decidedly preferable to yet another of those "where are you from and what do you do?" evenings. The very word "relationship"—which, by the way, I tried (and failed) to exclude from this book entirely— sounds ponderous and hits the ear with a dull, clinical thump. Even so, we're all looking for one—at bus stops, in continuing-education photography classes, next door, under rocks, everywhere.

You can't have much fun playing chess if you can't tell a pawn from a queen. In the same way, courtship is less exhilarating if you don't know the rules. What, finally, should you do when Felix asks you to dinner, spends the entire evening regaling you with stories of his divorce and then presents you with the check? What does it mean when Wendy invites you to the country for the weekend and asks her old boyfriend to join you for dinner on Saturday night? How should you respond and what should you think when Joe says he loves you? Since it's likely from all we know that many of us are going to spend much of our lives courting and dealing with just such questions, we might as well have a clear idea of what we want and can expect from courtship. How many *Gilligan's Island* reruns can you take, after all?

I wonder if it occurred to the Romantic poets that more cynical generations would think of their vision of the world as sentimental? Perhaps later generations will look back on us and think us sentimental romantics, too. We're obsessed with love, and with giving and receiving pleasure. For all our experience to the contrary, we are fervent believers in happiness. We still trust, if secretly and cautiously, in fair damsels, knights in shining armor, happily-ever-afters. And we're still far from the mechanical stage Huxley describes in *Brave New World*, where women wear contraceptives on their belts the way warriors once sported scalps.

Until such a time as we can, the way oysters do, reproduce easily, without sex, we're locked for better or worse into the rituals of courtship. And the current state of these rituals? Surprisingly like what Francis Bacon said about behavior some three hundred years ago:

> Behavior is a garment of a mind and ought to have the conditions of a garment. For first, it ought to be made in fashion; secondly, it should not be too curious or costly; thirdly, it ought to be so framed as best to set forth any virtue of the mind and supply and hide any deformity; and lastly, and above all, it ought not to be strait, so as to confine the mind and interfere with its freedom in business and action.

Chapter Two

Measuring Love

A PASSAGE in Raymond Carver's story "What We Talk About When We Talk About Love" haunts me. Terri, recalling the man she lived with before she lived with Mel, her current lover, says, "People are different, Mel. Sure, sometimes he may have acted crazy. Okay. But he loved me. In his own way, maybe, but he loved me. There was love there, Mel. Don't say there wasn't." From the vehemence of her defense, it's clear that she's not quite certain that even she believes what she's saying, and Mel probably doesn't believe her, either. So what does she really mean when she talks about love? What do any of us mean?

Because it's never been an easy question to answer, we've tended to avoid confusion by finding ways to verify and label love, often by letting a convenient and static symbol stand for the complex and fluid emotion of love. Centuries ago in Wales, for example, it was the custom for a young man to carve an elaborate wooden spoon for the girl he wanted to marry. Once the two were spooning, the status of the romance was clear to all concerned.

The practical Yankees were less subtle, and not much given to symbolism. When a young New England couple decided to marry, they posted a notice on the town bulletin board. Everyone, including the governor, was expected to acknowledge and endorse the marriage with at least a few ears of corn. Thus was love measured in simpler times.

Until recently, when young people not even out of their teens thought ahead to marriage after the third date or so they quantified what they believed to be their enduring love with ID bracelets, class rings, varsity jackets or some other recognizable gift. When these same kids went off to college and found another enduring love, the young woman displayed her beau's intentions by wearing his fraternity pin or the lavaliere he gave her, just as the two would later hang their diplomas on the wall to prove they were ready to face the world. To make the meaning of these symbols plain to anyone who might not know how to translate the code, they would further explain the situation by saying they were "engaged to be engaged."

We still make a public statement when it comes to marriage, with a wedding ring and possibly an engagement ring as well, along with, for some, an announcement of the marriage in the local paper. (A friend of mine, obviously aware of how much it matters to measure love in public, once said that when she got married she wouldn't settle for a normal-sized announcement, but would take out a full-page ad in the *New York Times*.)

If we still depend on such symbols to tell the world that we're married, there are few adult counterparts to Welsh spoons and ID bracelets to display the stages of adult courtship, to say publicly for us: "See, somebody loves me. I'm this far along in loving, and in being loved." And yet most of us crave tangible proof to show the world—and ourselves: "Somebody loves me." You can keep all your ticket stubs, pressed flowers and yellowing dance programs in a dusty old scrapbook, but for most of us it's not enough to be well loved if it's all in private.

We don't much go in for the beeline-to-the-altar approach to courtship anymore—it's more like a labyrinth with hundreds of dead ends—and you can't really measure with traditional symbols the various steps along the way to love; there are simply too many steps now, going in too many directions.

When political systems collapse, citizens usually renounce their belief in the state itself and in the laws they once obeyed; the result is something close to chaos, or anarchy. When courtship is thrown into a similar state of anarchy, as it has been for us, the rules, the tangible symbols and even the language we have come to depend upon also lose their meaning. "No, no, my darling," sometimes means, "Yes, of course." Red sometimes means go—and a green light can mean herpes. When our customary ways of doing things give in to anarchy so, as a rule, do our emotions.

Thus when someone says, "I don't know where we stand," he or she is uttering more than a rhetorical complaint. When it comes to love, most of us truly don't have the remotest idea where we stand, and few ways to measure or determine it. Even if the two of you have discussed your "prospects" ad nauseum, as people in relationships these days seem to do, it's still a risk to assume from a passionate conversation one romantic, snowy evening that it's safe to tell your friends the next day, "Well, yes, Tony says he loves me more than he's ever loved anyone else."

To make the memory real, to validate the courtship, perhaps you should have had Tony put what he felt in writing.

Nearly all the "typical late-twentieth-century courtship case studies" that come immediately to mind seem to defy any kind of conventional courtship logic. There's Suzette who wants to marry Harvey one week, or so she believes, and then the next invests in a studio co-op which, no matter how many space-saving modules she might buy, will never hold her stationary bicycle and his portable jogging machine. Harvey's reaction is mingled anger and despair until, that is, he's distracted by a job offer in Indianapolis, six hundred miles away. (So not to keep you in suspense: All this took place for Harvey and Suzette a few months ago. Suzette's co-op deal feel through, Harvey turned down his job offer and still they're no closer to marriage—yet no less in love—than they were when this particular trauma took place.) But how could you pinpoint with a symbol how far Harvey and Suzette have come in their courtship? With most of our romances, you simply can't. Our circumstances and our emotions simply change too fast. Even the word "emotion" has its root in the word "motion."

Moreover, what kind of a symbol would work for us? The criterion for a courtship symbol, remember, is that it's easily recognized by everyone in one's immediate group. Most of us, if we take into account all our personal, professional and social roles, inhabit several overlapping and disparate groups: With all these roles, it's nearly impossible to choose a symbol that would be appropriate. As you'll see, Harvey and Suzette are pretty far along in their courtship (they're in about Chapter Ten). What could he possibly give her or she him to show the world where they stand—L. L. Bean boots? A windbreaker with the name of a bank on the back? An engraved coke spoon?

Embroidered blue jeans? Even if one of these made sense, the intended symbolism would be lost on an audience too preoccupied with where things stand in their own lives to pay attention.

Even so, the need to measure love persists. For example, I never fail to take the *Cosmo* romance quizzes ("How much does he *love* you? Test your romance I.Q.") every month, and I suspect I'm not the only one to puzzle over the questions, or *Cosmo* wouldn't be wasting its space issue after issue. Without symbols we can trust, we find it hard to be certain of love, just as we would find it hard to figure out what to do with a recipe that said throw in some sugar, baking soda and a bunch of chopped walnuts, without explaining what to do step by step, and what the results would be.

Now that we have no universally reliable courtship benchmarks, we tend to create our own as we go along. In the beginning of a romance, a Saturday night ranks higher than a Tuesday, and New Year's Eve and Memorial Day Weekend are Big Deals. Meeting your friend's friends is an honor of sorts, and meeting his or her children, as many people see it, is a sign of something serious. A woman whose lover sends her flowers at the office is, whether she likes it or not, the recipient of a traditional courtship symbol; even if *she* can't quite tell what he's trying to say with the tulips, her curious and gossip-prone colleagues will undoubtedly figure the whole thing out for her.

We also measure love by marking courtship time. Everyone has a private timetable (only partly conscious, I suspect) with which to determine whether a romance is on schedule. But time alone is not always a reliable symbol. If you say, "We've been seeing each other for a year now," you may be reflecting on a virtual lifetime while your confidante, judging from his or her own timetable and experience, may think you mean an affair that's barely off the ground. House keys, a corner of the closet, the use of a drawer, "permission" to answer your lover's telephone—these, too, might be symbols of a deepening commitment. But unlike the firm reality of, say, a class ring, these still do not mean the same things to everyone—nor are they all *public* symbols: You can't carry around your borrowed drawer—and so we're still in a symbolic quandary. What was Grace really saying when she told Chip he could leave an extra shirt and some underwear in her bottom drawer? Was there any symbolic meaning when Frank told Charlotte she could use his beloved BMW while he was in Houston on business?

I heard from a friend the story of Rachel, who was once having some trouble figuring out where she stood with Jonathan. She had been seeing him for some months. During the week they spent a lot of time together, but there were summer weekends when he'd mysteriously disappear, something about visiting friends. She wondered whether he was seeing someone else, or if he didn't feel the way about her that she did about him. (In another day, in a smaller town, he couldn't even have gotten away with this. But today, in the big city, it happens all the time.) Still, he was attentive, she liked him and she looked forward to celebrating her birthday with him one Friday night early in September. When he arrived for dinner, he brought her one of the small, plastic-potted rhododendron plants that were for sale at the flower wagon on the corner of her street. It didn't hurt her that the plant cost only a couple of dollars. What hurt her was the symbolic—and real—cruelty that his gift represented. Here was a symbol with a vengeance.

In other cases we can over-measure love. I talked to a man who started going out with a woman a short time ago, warning her from the beginning that he was still preoccupied with his last affair and not looking for anything "heavy." For Christmas she gave him a set of toiletries, complete with designer shaving paraphernalia (of all things), to use when he stayed at her house. He had bought her two record albums. Under the circumstances, her gift was wildly inappropriate, an over-measurement of his feelings for her, and he was uncomfortable enough to stop seeing her entirely.

In the absence of such standardized courtship gifts as those old fraternity pins, the gifts we choose for each other have taken on heavy symbolic meaning, for we have no real guidelines beyond our always dubious common sense to tell us what kind of gift measures the appropriate amount of love, and when. If you're not absolutely certain about the role you play in his or her life, any occasion where custom decrees a gift is going to make you wish you were a mind reader. What if you think you're pretty far along and you're willing to invest in a food processor that the two of you can use together, but he's not as committed and gives you a dumb Shetland crewneck? Gifts, apart from those that imparted symbolic statements, meant less in earlier times when they were prescribed by the book. A Victorian woman could pretty well predict when she'd be sent carnations and when she would move up to one of those familiar, chastely inscribed slender volumes of verse. Our worry comes from knowing that our gifts hold the power to say too much for us — or too little.

Casting about for symbols, we have struck on one potent phrase to verify that we are courting: I love you. For Jane Austen, the avowal of love always pops up in the last chapter, just before the wedding; in our own jumbled romances we get to that point earlier, and more often.

The Germans have thirty separate words for kiss, expressing every innuendo of the gesture, but we have only one for love, and it serves to describe our attachment to chocolate-chip ice cream and Aunt Nancy as well as to express our deepest romantic feelings. Formerly a man would be careful about expressing passionate love, because such an expression amounted to a promise—and to a wife. Now we have looser rules for saying I love you.

Many of us regard the phrase as sacred, but still, among people I've interviewed, a number concede that on being told, "I love you," the only civilized and gracious way to respond is to return the compliment—unless you want to end the thing right there. Others feel that it's okay to offer the phrase, as they would a compliment, when it suits the moment, or the mood. The word "love," then, connotes not an absolute state of feeling but a matter of degree, and almost any degree.

Saying "I love you" can mean "I like you"; "I'm having a good time, aren't you?"; "Yes, we're lovers"; "I love you by my own definition." Or it can mean the real thing, whatever that is. Early on in a relationship, what it most often means, I think, is that we're not in love but "in hope." Everyone complains these days that so many people are afraid to get involved, but for those of us who need to love and feel loved in order to feel alive the reverse is also true: Often we are too eager to find ourselves in love. Stendhal said, "It needs only a very small quantity of hope to beget love," and now that courtship is a lifelong process, hope does indeed seem to spring eternal for us.

Some time ago I talked with a neighbor at his apartment—a salesman in his mid-thirties. As he sat on his tweed sofa eating a supper of warmed-up frozen waffles and drinking a beer, he talked about love and courtship. There's a point, he feels, possibly after first- or second-time sex, when the only words to fill the silence are, "I love you." "You can get around it, I suppose, but saying 'I love you' just seems nicer, it takes away the doubts of the moment. Love doesn't mean forever. You can hope it does, but mostly it doesn't."

When to say "I love you" is one thing; what to believe when someone says it to you is another. To accept at face value a phrase that has so many faces is harder than it first appears. Experience will teach you that the meaning of the phrase changes many times throughout a relationship, and throughout a lifetime. Many of us who have all the time in the world to experiment with love are, ironically, in too much of a hurry to "wait love out" and see what will happen. Some people will greet the first "I love you" with suspicion or a cynical denial; others will grab onto the phrase like snapping turtles.

The best you can hope for from the first mention of love is the reassurance that you both are, for the moment at least, just where you should be. At worst you'll find yourself asking yourself questions that during the early stages of love are impossible to answer: "You love me? What can you possibly mean by that?" "What on earth am I saying?" "What do these words have to do with my life?" "What about tomorrow?" "And what about James, Fred and Bob?" While it isn't always safe to assume anything, what you should probably assume from the first mention of love is that it comes from an impulse that's both genuine and generous. It may require a semantic adjustment in our notions about courtship to accept the fact that when we talk about love these days we're not necessarily talking about forever.

Just as the meaning of love has shifted, the responsibilities we attach to love have also changed. There might be such a thing as free sex, but the flower children of the Sixties were wrong: There is no free love. As we know from experience, love is an enormous responsibility and requires a great deal of attention and work. By instinct we can usually tell whether we're living up to the standards of love—and the standards, the responsibilities, grow as we pass from one stage of love to the next.

It's common, when a love fails to last forever, for us to assume that we've failed somehow in our responsibilities, that possibly we're not capable of true love or that we don't deserve it. Or we might believe instead that we've been deceived or misled. Most of us try to make some sense of endings by enumerating reasons and by casting blame, frequently by blaming ourselves. But if we are to succeed in adjusting our ideas about courtship to our times, we have to learn to be generous not only in accepting love for what it is, but also when love ends.

A man I went out with for a while a long time ago once said to me, "I think we have a real chance together"—his own way of saying that he might grow to love me. Had he talked about love at that point, I would have been pleased but confused or possibly not very trusting; his fresh new expression, on the other hand, thrilled me. As it turned out, we didn't have a chance at all, for reasons neither of us could have predicted, but the affair ended as carefully and beautifully as it had begun. Now we're friends, and whatever affection existed between us is a bond that strengthens the friendship.

One of the tragedies of our time is that we often don't realize that time spent loving need never be time wasted. We're getting there—many divorces are amicable, and many romances really do end in close friendships—but we still have a way to go. One woman I interviewed grew tearful as she repeated what her companion of three years had said to her the evening they broke up: "Well, that's that. Three years down the drain." With those words he tarnished and denied the love that once had mattered to them more than anything else. Moreover, he tarnished and denied what would one day have become an enchanted memory.

Confusing as the pursuit of love is today, it's comforting to remember not only that love *never* has been easy, but also that we're still test-marketing the idea that romance and a happily-ever-after ending can be packaged successfully together. Unlike anger, an emotion whose essence remains the same from century to century—even if ways to vent it might change—the definition of love is always affected by the times. The Western love myth, which still dominates our imaginations, dates from the twelfth century, the age of chivalry, when love was defined entirely differently from the way we think of it now.

Eight centuries ago, Europeans didn't need a computer to figure out who would marry whom. Marriage was governed by one set of rules, and love by another. The rules of chivalry—the courtship etiquette, songs and all, that kept things lively for the residents of Camelot—were a code for love outside marriage, rules, in effect, which legitimated the practice of adultery. Love at that time didn't lead to marriage; love led, in fact, *away* from marriage.

This chivalric code tested human will and strength not by how many acts of sexual intercourse could be consummated successfully in one evening but by the ability of the human spirit to prevail over lowly sexual instincts. Human will being what it is, chastity belts, or Florentine girdles, were invented soon after the rules of chivalry were tested and found wanting.

The code of chivalry was complicated, and not every knight could qualify. The virtues toward which the perfect knight aspired included courage, charity, loyalty, spontaneity in giving, humility and hospitality, along with devotion to the service of love. Once he chose a woman as the object of his devotion, the knight would spend the rest of his life perfecting himself in order to win her favor and her love. To make his pursuit of love even more challenging, the knight usually chose a married woman to put on his pedestal.

From the lady's point of view, of course, it was nice to have a knight around the castle. She had the children and the serfs to worry about, and it wasn't easy running that big house. She probably didn't find her marriage, which had been made with no regard to the vicissitudes of passion or love, terribly fulfilling. Marriage, she knew, was mainly to keep the species alive, the social classes intact and the property where it belonged—in the hands of the right families and their legitimate offspring. Lords married ladies, and serfs, once they reached breeding age, were paired up by their lords and masters with other suitable serfs. Love had nothing to do with it, no matter what your station.

The lady's husband (the lord) wasn't even much of a companion—most lords were away on business all the time. He'd stop in at home now and then, pick up his mail, polish his armor and ride off again, to trade spices perhaps, to join the Crusades or to serenade a lady of his own. Even his religion didn't keep him at home, because marriage at the time was a secular matter, having more to do with property than with God. Oddly, the Bible calls for a decree of divorcement, but no certificate of marriage—and marriage didn't have to be blessed by the clergy until the sixteenth century.

So the idea of such love triangles suited all parties concerned. For the lord, having a few errant knights watch over his affairs made perfect sense: He could feel easier about matters at home while he was away, and could pretty well tell if the knights and his wife were following the rules. The knight, for his part, got free room and board at a castle—and could spend all his time following around his one true love. The lady, call her Lady A, who really had the best of all possible worlds, had a script for ideal love that must have gone something like this: "I will marry Lord A, to whom I will devote my domestic life. I'll have his children, care for his domain while he's crusading, be his earthly mate. But I deserve to have some fun, too. While he's away, there's no harm in playing around with Sir B—as long as we're careful not to go too far. He writes lovely ballads for me, and performs daring feats on my behalf. He's handy and eager to help out, and will work with me to have the castle in order when Lord A comes home." In a time when the social classes were top-heavy with men, and there weren't enough real ladies to go around, this arrangement made a lot of sense, however peculiar it might sound to us now.

Each subsequent generation has revised the script to suit itself, but marriages such as Lady A's are hardly a thing entirely of the past. Even today, though the custom is under debate, a bride-price is exacted in some parts of the Middle East, thereby giving the girl's parents veto power over inappropriate suitors and, until the mid-Sixties, most Japanese parents arranged proper marriages for their sons and daughters quite apart from how the young people felt about it. In 1981, one Iranian couple committed suicide when their parents refused to let them marry, and we all know that even the most liberated American parent is not immune to plotting a way for little Mary to grow up and marry rich Beauford Peep.

But for the most part, the script for ideal love eight centuries after the courtiers shows that Lord A and Sir B have become one and the same person. What we expect from ideal love is more than King Arthur and his friends ever did: "Here is Harry, who will share the responsibilities of my condo, empty the garbage and be supportive of me as I am supportive of him. We'll both work hard to pay for the life-style we would like to have. In addition, we love each other very much and will continue to do so absolutely. Our sex life will be constant and good, and we will always have fun on weekends. We will never be bored. Harry will never get so much on my nerves that I want to scream simply because he drinks orange juice directly from the container, and I can live the rest of my life without telling him that his best friend Al is a creep."

We now invest both our practical and romantic resources in those we choose to love, and we ask much in return: From those we court we hope for immediate, intuitive love; romance; perfect sex and sentiment. We also want someone who helps out, pays half of everything and is fun to be around. We also talk about wanting honesty and open communication (whatever that is) in a relationship—but actually what we want is a perfect love that does not have to be analyzed and scrutinized at every turn.

Romantic love is a fragile bond, and the courtiers handled it delicately. They never asked as much from it as we do. But because many of us can no longer count on close families and reliable communities to nourish us spiritually, and because we haven't much confidence anymore in what the future will bring, we keep adding a little here and a little there to what we expect when we talk about love. There's an inadvertent double entendre when we say that we want to make love work. Not only do we mean that we want a love affair to work out happily, but never before has this fragile emotion been expected to work so hard as it does for us today. From our therapists, TV shows and how-to books, we have come to believe that endless happiness is not only possible—a revolutionary thought in itself—but something to which each of us has the right. But how can we figure out just what happiness is ("Test your happiness I.Q."), and when do we know that enough love is enough? "There was love there, Mel. Don't say there wasn't."

In his classic *Love in the Western World*, the Swiss philosopher Denis de Rougement makes the convincing argument that because we Westerners have never really bothered to define happiness in a pragmatic way, we will never find it. We certainly won't find it in romantic love, which is ephemeral, he says, or in marriage, which in our culture has come to depend so much on romantic love.

Convincing as de Rougement's theory is, he still misses a point. More things are possible than this practical philosopher imagines. We all know that few things are more beautiful than two people long in love sharing a private joke or a touch on the arm, or simply looking at each other with a smile when they meet. This is the kind of love each of us hopes for, and this is why we go on courting, no matter how many times we may have been disappointed.

My friend Catherine, who is almost forty and has been in and out of love many times, knows what she's talking about when she talks about love. Recently she returned from the happy occasion of her parents' fiftieth wedding-anniversary celebration. "It was just like when I was a kid," she said. "You have to clear your throat when you walk into my parents' kitchen at home, because you never know what's going to be going on in there."

Chapter Three

The Players, and the Games

BEFORE CONSIDERING the stages of courtship and what to expect from each one, we should define just who it is who's doing the courting—and where and how all this so-called "action" is taking place. In earlier, more stable times, both men and women were trained in certain romantic formalities: The boy says this, the girl says that and here's what will happen. What about today, though, when men and women don't operate under separate sets of rules, when standards of behavior that used to be black and white have become something more like camouflage green?

Those good old days of courtship, when boys were supposed to be boys and girls unquestionably were girls, had another advantage. Orderly societies laid out and monitored rules (rules again) that said, "This activity is reserved for courtship," or, "This one is not." Supervised parlor visits and debutante balls were okay; meeting a stranger at the butcher shop was not. Romantic stragglers were never left wondering whether they should have exchanged more than a friendly smile at the fund-raising campaign, or a wan expression of commiseration at the Smokenders orientation session—they would have *known* these occasions were not courtship opportunities. We, however, lack both an up-front courtship etiquette and the guidance of a society that sees to it that we meet each other in a conventional or prescribed way.

It is, then, if you think about it, no surprise that even though more of us than ever before are single, a prevailing complaint is: "I never meet anybody." It's as if we're caught in a game of blindman's bluff, bumping into each other without realizing who's behind the blindfold. No one seems to meet anyone anymore. But because I understand the complaint all too well, I simply can't accept the notion that we're all hopelessly antisocial or maladjusted. Something else must be wrong. Possibly it's a mistake to play the courtship game without rules, and without a wise leader to teach us what's what: "Okay, Salmonella, this guy here is about to become interested in you, and even though this is a health club and you're supposed to be here on behalf of your cellulite, it's in perfectly good taste to put down your barbells, smile back at him and agree to one of those disgusting Orange Vitalities at the juice bar after your workout."

Sophisticated and experienced as we're all supposed to be these days, my guess is that you're much likelier to recognize a would-be mugger from half a block away than you are to notice a potential date staring you in the face from a distance of three inches.

Surely it must be easier for parents to explain sex to their kids these days than it is for them to explain how courtship works. There's little variation on the theme that the-man's-penis-goes-into-the-woman's-vagina. It's much more difficult to understand the fine line of difference between "meeting someone" and being "picked up." Or how and when to be friendly—and how and when to be *friendly*. Or, and this is particularly baffling to women, what distinguishes assertiveness from aggressiveness and how to get up the courage to be assertive in the first place. Romance has always been thought an art, and we simply don't study or practice it as such anymore. But tackling the mechanics of courtship requires first tackling the question of how men and women are supposed to act.

In my interviews and on my questionnaires I introduced the subject of courtship by asking, "What is a lady?" and "What is a gentleman?" To the first question, one man responded, "Don't know, never met one," and from another I heard, "I thought this interview was supposed to be about fucking." Some people defined ladies and gentlemen as extinct or endangered species—"A lady was..." or "A gentleman is anyone over eighty." Others distinguished by generation, "My father was a gentleman; I'm just a guy."

Overwhelmingly, though, most people, even today, have clear feelings on the subject. A lady has self-respect and respect for others; she treats all people, men and women, in the same way. She is kind and generous, she has integrity. A gentleman? "The same." We have uprooted many of our customs, traditions and even ideals, but we still place honor and virtue among the most prized qualities to which men and women can aspire.

What's new is that good manners are no longer sex-specific.

Being a lady today has nothing to do with how many pairs of white gloves you have, and a gentleman has more to worry about than whether to walk on the curbside and risk a speeding bus splashing mud on his brand-new linen suit. We've all but dispensed with arbitrary edicts listing how ladies behave in Column A and how gentlemen do in Column B—a breakthrough in etiquette, most will agree. Yet noble and decent as this new doctrine of unisex manners sounds, it still leaves many of us pondering such difficult philosophical questions as, "Who's going to pay for this dinner?"

At the turn of this century, according to the etiquette of the age, a gentleman knew that if he wanted to call on a lady he had to do so between four and seven if he lived in the East, and later in the evening if he lived in the South or West. He stayed no longer than thirty minutes. He could not be introduced to a woman without first, through a complicated grapevine arrangement, receiving her permission, and once he met her, he never allowed her to carry so much as a "package, umbrella or wrap." It was in "wretched taste" for a young girl to loiter with a man, to stop for a chat on a street corner, to use slang or to fidget.

The lady was also aware that even if there were no servant around, she was not to help a caller with his wraps ("Nice but socially uninstructed girls lay themselves open to severe criticism through exactly such mistaken notions."), and realized that "when a young girl allows a young man to call her by her first name, unless engaged to him, she cheapens his regard for her by just so much." When dining out, both parties had to remember that a "man's ideas as to appropriate food are more reliable than those of a woman." Indeed!

Young people learned these rules, I assume, in the same way we learn today that wearing your jeans too short makes you look as if you're going to a flood; that you must never admit on a first date that you'd like to be married by your next birthday; that it's not particularly chic to overdo the subject of astrology and that it's best not to confide in a potential lover that you sleep with a teddy bear. The rules one needs to know to get by in a culture, the definitions of appropriate and inappropriate behavior, become so much a part of us by the time we need to use them that they're almost second nature. We learn our manners in the same ways people have always learned them: from our parents and our peers, from observation and simply from living in a certain world. Where the manners of courtship are concerned, we don't learn to be ladies and gentlemen—the words imply a chasm between the sexes that no longer exists. What we learn now is to be people.

This androgyny, a fusing of masculine and feminine traits, has shattered the old ideals of romantic dominance and submission and marks a real upheaval in relations between men and women—and thus an upheaval in the sexual pecking order. Japanese women, for example, once they married, used to shave their eyebrows, a symbol of their beauty, as a gesture of subservience to their husbands. For similar reasons, Egyptian women would cut their hair after marriage; Orthodox Jewish women still do. Here in the West, although most women managed to survive with eyebrows and hair intact, they wore wedding veils, the traditional symbol of deference to their grooms, and knew full well the restrictions marriage imposed upon them.

Burdensome as the old rules were for women, men didn't have it so easy, either. Think what a simple evening out must have been like for your grandfather: saving up his money in anticipation of a date, going through the humiliation of being checked out by the girl's parents, picking her up, opening all those doors, choosing the restaurant and selecting what she would eat, picking up the tab, rushing home to meet her curfew, a limp handshake at the door. And then, after all that work, at the end of the evening he was required to thank her for the pleasure of her company.

In 1959, sociologist Ervin Goffman wrote, "American college girls did, and no doubt do, play down their intelligence, skills and determinitiveness when in the presence of datable boys, thereby manifesting a profound psychic discipline in spite of their reputation for flightiness." Though Goffman was trying to make a sociological point, his comment was tantamount at the time to etiquette advice.

Even as recently as 1974, in the paperback edition of *Amy Vanderbilt's Everyday Etiquette*, the author advised the woman in need of guidance on what to do while her date was checking their coats in a restaurant (presumably the woman was just standing around feeling foolish): "Your feelings of helplessness can be a great social asset in this instance. Just allow your date to take full charge."

I'm no genius, but I can think of countless better answers. Check your own coat, or advise against checking coats in the first place (might be cold, high risk of theft, quicker getaway). Go directly to the table, or go to the ladies' room. Read a magazine at the bar, or drop a contact lens on the floor so you can look for it. Don't wear a coat. Androgyny is about options, and about never having to feel helpless.

Unisex clothing and hair stylists, make-up for men, the ideal if not the reality of equality in business, even male doctors cloning away in their laboratories to create life, as women have always been able to do right in their beds—these are all outward signs of androgyny. But it's a mistake to think that this kind of "cosmetic" androgyny is new. In the seventeenth century, Puritans in America were enraged by dandies who wore lovelocks, long curls extending almost to their shoulders, because they made men look like women. Harvard first banned long hair in

1655, centuries before the Beatles, and many evenings were given over to the argument about whether those enormous powdered wigs gentlemen wore were decadent, in much the same way that "traditionalists" grumbled during the Sixties about not being able to tell the boys from the girls. (I'd always wondered about Yankee Doodle calling his feather "macaroni"—I pictured a cap with a big noodle jutting out from it at a jaunty angle. But a macaroni in those days was another name for a dandy, and the way the song was first written Mr. Doodle called himself, and not the feather, a macaroni.)

The androgyny that's important today concerns a more fundamental change in the way we live, the manners we practice, the means by which we set up our relations with the opposite sex. Men and women open doors for each other, help with coats, bundles, expenses, chores, children, entertaining. We go out of our way to listen to each other, to give those we care about emotional boosts, to be considerate sexually. What we're aiming for now, it seems to me, is an etiquette of self-determinism, being gracious and giving because we want to be and not because as ladies and gentlemen we're supposed to be. It no longer makes sense to regard man as breadwinner and woman as domestic orchestra leader. What attracts us to each other in our world are factors that are harder to pinpoint than the old roles were: companionship, humor, sex, common interests, the perfect emotional match.

For us the ideal woman, what used to be called a lady, is a daunting creature. She knows how to make a living and manage her affairs. She can go to the movies alone, travel by herself, be, if she chooses, a single mother, buy her own home or car, master any discipline she likes. At the same time, she's supposed to be as feminine as she always was, keep her body and mind in tip-top shape, wear designer clothes and knit afghans for dozens of her closest friends at Christmas. She is matched in her powers only by the contemporary ideal man, the former gentleman, who is custom-tailored for her. He, too, has a thriving career and myriad interests on the side. He knows that there won't necessarily be a woman around to tend to his meals, his home and his laundry, so he's learned to cope with those details on his own, when he's not at the office enjoying his fulfilling and lucrative career, that is. He, too, has to look good, stay in shape, be a super-parent, blow-dry his hair and stay in tune with his feelings.

But these jolly hybrids with all their accomplishments—these paragons who make you want to crawl into bed and take a nap—aren't really people at all but ideals. As has always been true, most of us regard it as something of a triumph simply to make it through the day without major catastrophe. It's not easy being a woman, it's not easy being a man; now that we have to play the roles of both, it's a wonder that anyone can stay awake long enough to watch the eleven o'clock news. And it's no wonder that the question, "Who's going to pay for this dinner?" is still unanswered.

We've all heard a lot recently about role reversal, an idea that is pretty easy to grasp: the man with the smudge of flour on his cheek kissing his wife-with-a-briefcase goodbye in the morning; the woman in the Harvey's Bristol Cream commercial inviting the unsuspecting, innocent man over to her sumptuous apartment for a seduction. The everyday androgyny, the twenty-four hour self-reliance we're talking about here, however, has more to do with bumping heads when you're both trying a passionate embrace, or trying to open doors for each other. Or, if you both like to cook, with arguments over what to serve for dinner. Or with a stalemate in your plans to live together because neither of you will give up your apartment. Typical androgynous conversations go something like: "Where d'ya wanna eat tonight?" "I don't care, where d'you?" Or, "What do you mean? I paid for the tickets last time," an exchange I heard in a movie-ticket line the other day. The up side of androgyny is that if you're really leaning toward pizza you have a pretty good chance of getting it. The down side is that there is no one to take charge if you can't decide between pizza and sushi. And because androgyny is so new to courtship, it leaves us wondering who's supposed to do what— etiquette by trial and error.

I suspect that men and women have always had a soft spot in their hearts for members of the other sex with an androgynous streak. The women most attractive in Victorian novels are those with an adventurous gleam in their eyes and a defiant way of tossing chestnut manes of hair in rebellion against their mothers' admonitions about what is ladylike. The most appealing men have often been those with a gentle, even feminine side. Mellors, Lady Chatterley's famous lover, is unquestionably manly, but his attraction lies in his gentleness, his sympathy for Lady C.'s soul. But when the going got rough for these fictional trailblazers, they could always retreat into their "real" roles: The defiant young heroine could get married, and Mellors could find someone else's game to keep. It's too late for us to retreat into the old roles, and most of us wouldn't choose to go back if we could.

There is a passage in *Madame Bovary* in which Emma asks about her husband, Charles: "Wasn't it a man's role, though, to know everything? Shouldn't he be an expert on all kinds of things, able to initiate you into the intensities of passion, the refinements of life, all the mysteries?" That was a pretty heavy trip to lay on poor Charles. Emma was a tough cookie, and her disingenuousness still got her into plenty of trouble—today she'd be hopeless.

Our relations today draw their energy from sharing, as Emma might say, the expertise on all kinds of things, and not from a rigid division of romantic labor.

In a game of chess, the queen carries more power than the king. She can move around the board in any direction, over any number of squares. Although the king can also navigate in any direction, he can only move one square at a time. Androgyny has done for courtship what giving kings power equal to queens would do for chess. We've had to re-think the game of courtship, the strategies, even the outcome. That's enough of an upheaval in itself, yet there's still another change with which we must reckon in order to understand how courtship works today.

With the same intensity of purpose that drives ants to build ant hills and salmon to swim upstream to lay their eggs, human beings have, throughout history, gone about ensuring that men and women would be paired up in an orderly, ritualistic way. In most cultures, the responsibility of arranging suitable marriages has fallen upon tribal leaders or upon the parents, who traditionally have paid the same kind of attention to the pomp and ceremony of courtship that bookies pay to Kentucky Derby odds. But what happens in a culture like ours, when the parents are retired and living in Florida, on their second and third marriages themselves—or simply too busy with their own romances to bother with those of their children? Who's in charge of seeing that a Nobel Prize-winning scientist of thirty-five finds a husband before she's too old to have children?

Cotillion, a French word for petticoat, was first used to describe an extravagant ball in the eighteenth century. Imagine the scene: the clatter as the coaches begin to arrive; footmen carefully unpacking ladies and gentlemen from their carriages, as if they were jewels. The polished dance floor in readiness, the light from hundreds of candles refracted in the sparkling crystal prisms of elaborate chandeliers. The guests themselves, women in silks, satins, watered taffeta, the men impeccable in black breeches, ruffled white shirts and frockcoats. Toward the end of the evening, the orchestra picks up the pace of its waltzes and the older men and women retire to the sidelines to watch the young people, who by now are paired off and dancing giddily, the hems of lacy petticoats sometimes visible as young girls, flushed with the first possibility of romance, swirl about the floor....

Such scenes are marvelous centerpieces for novels and movies, but even in real life these parties, scaled of course to social class, played a key role in the social matrix: These parties were society's way of arranging that boy would meet girl, and their parents' way of assuring that the family, and by extension the species, would go on.

Marriageable kids were also hauled around to all sorts of cultural events and displayed at dinner parties. For those who turned out to be a little more difficult to marry off, there were distant relatives (who presumably knew a whole new crop of eligibles) to visit, and summer excursions—the spa at Baden-Baden was a legendary singles' meeting ground in the 1800s—on which to continue the hunt. Getting rid of these kids was as important to parents as selling merchandise is to a shopkeeper—and every salesman knows the value of good display. Daughters, who at best were expected to contribute a mean hand with a darning needle, were harder to dispense with. Their education was their preparation for marriage—rigorous lessons in charm and domesticity, learning to play the parlor piano. Dresses and dowries were, for the parents, investments. Sons learned a trade, of course, and the rudiments of social grace. Today's parents, lacking faith in marriage themselves and more concerned with their children's economic future, would rather they find a job than a spouse.

"Yeah, great," you're probably thinking. "That's fine, but what about me? It's almost the weekend, and nobody's arranged a cotillion on my behalf. And the one person I don't want to go out with is Aunt Tillie's bridge partner's son."

Without traditional ways to match us up, and without families who feel compelled to see that we're settled before they go on to other things, we are, whether we realize it or not, busily contriving a whole new set of courtship institutions of our own, taking matters into our own hands, so to speak.

Even a generation ago, before alienation came into fashion, parents still took a firm hand in guiding the courtship of their young. High school proms, college formals, country-club dances and such were set up to ensure that like would meet like. Even now a few of these persist as nostalgic rituals or as entertainment, but they no longer carry the commitment of purpose characteristic of earlier times.

Perhaps the last bastion of this kind of conventional courtship were soda shops, the kind we used to see in the old TV sitcoms, where "teens," under the benevolent eye of the soda jerk—who always had a kind word and a free Coke for the broken-hearted—would fraternize to the tunes on the jukebox. Often Ricky Nelson's father, the amiable Ozzie, would stop by to check up on the proceedings, since presumably he never had anything else to do in the afternoon. The soda shops don't work anymore, of course; so where do we meet to court?

The idea that we live in an impersonal society isn't new; ask anyone who has ever tried to reason with a computer or the phone company. Even courtship, the most personal of institutions, has not been unaffected by the impersonality that has reached so many areas of our lives.

Our families once saw to our social lives; we now rely on our friends, our professional colleagues and ourselves. Naturally, the people we know don't watch out for us as carefully as a doting mama would, but the circle of friends and acquaintances we all nurture will inevitably play a big part in whom we end up courting.

Shadchanim were Talmudic scholars who until the last century raised extra money for themselves by serving as matchmakers. The "Matchmaker, matchmaker, make me a match," from *Fiddler on the Roof* is just such a *shadchan.* Hired by the girl's parents, these moonlighters would advertise in Yiddish newspapers for suitors and, when the replies came in, would send the young fellows over for an interview. When the right one came along they got paid. Immigrants, far from homes where they knew virtually every young man (and his parents) who might do for their daughters, made special use of this service.

For those of us courting today, our friends help serve as *shadchanim*—for free. Formally we call the custom a blind date, a legacy from the days when parents arranged such meetings. More casually, we invite our unmatched friends to dinners and parties and outings, in the hope that they will find each other on their own, as a boy or girl at a cotillion years ago might have found his or her one true love. And because we so often meet our lovers through our friends, a whole new etiquette for friends and lovers has evolved, just as there was once a set of rules that told parents how to act around their children's romantic friends. Now we need answers to such questions as: Can I invite both Mark and Barbara to dinner without seeming too obvious, and should I tell them what I'm doing first? I'd like to ask my friend Cindy and her boyfriend, Dennis, to visit for the weekend—shall I call them separately? If Clare's friend Susan comes to dinner with Clare and me, how should I ask her for her share of the bill? Now that I'm divorced, how will the people I used to see together with my ex-wife react to my date? And so on. (Chapter Nine is about friends and lovers.)

The office, too, as everyone knows, now plays a part in courtship, even though we still subscribe to the taboo of office relations, calling them "incestuous" because the company has become somehow like a family, and romances between family members are of course off limits.

I asked the people I interviewed about going out with business associates, and the response was largely, "A terrible idea," "Never get involved with someone from your office," "Nothing but trouble." The obvious next question was, "Have you ever done it?" As often as not the answer was, "Yeah, that's how I know."

Yet there are some people who feel that office romance is unavoidable or possibly even desirable. Where else can you find someone who so readily understands your interests, shares so many of the same jokes, keeps your schedule, knows just what you're talking about when you mention your work? Even putting all that aside, if you're cooped up in the office all the time where else will you even have the chance to meet someone?

While the unwritten policies (there is no law here) for dealing with love in the office vary from company to company, even from profession to profession, and while some colleagues are more generous about such things than others, I suspect that this will become an issue of increasing procedural and legal importance over the next few years. It's pointless and illogical for a company to make a perfectly competent female accountant leave her job in shame simply because she falls in love with the company lawyer. Nor should he have to go searching for another company. Assuming that the business at hand goes on uninterrupted, an office relationship should not necessarily be made to seem as tacky and illicit as the legendary affair between the housewife and the milkman.

A note here about discretion. Back when romances were straightforward and mainly involved people who were young and had always been single, there was little need to behave clandestinely, unless there was something expressly forbidden about the liaison. The circumstances for love among adults, however, frequently are not so simple. Men and women who are separated but not yet divorced; those with children; business associates; friends who aren't yet certain they want to make a public statement about their feelings—even the most respectable affairs today may at one time or another require some discretion. A friend once showed me a greeting card featuring on the front a drawing of one of those fake noses with eyeglasses attached and the single word "Discreet." The inscription inside was a series of Byzantine instructions for meeting: one party would leave the lights on, the phone off the hook and sneak out the back door dressed in a chicken suit; the other would appear at a Moonie meeting. There are ways to build discretion into your friendship without sacrificing either your sense of humor or your dignity.

Outside the office and away from your friends, the possibilities for courtship are endless—and endlessly bewildering. For one thing, there's the romance industry: the singles' bars, resorts, clubs, condominium developments. There are numerous organizations like Single Booklovers, Parents without Partners, even one I read about recently for people who don't like to eat alone. A Boston entrepreneur has started a matchmaking service for herpes victims; there are special magazines for singles. Big-time computer dating services have replaced small-time matchmakers, and for the truly purposeful there are highly paid dating consultants and companies that set up video "screenings" for potential partners.

For all the attention this industry gets, however, and for all the talk about the glamorous singles' life, I think that this scene is only a peripheral part of the courtship that really goes on today. Many people I talked to and most of the people I know have never even *been* to a singles' bar—and among those who have, the suggestion that they go in order to get (in a word) laid amounts to an insult.

The singles' business has its logic. We do live in a fast-track impersonal society where there isn't an orderly way to meet. Many of us live among strangers. These businesses exist to bring unpaired people together—not so different, really, from the service the Welcome Wagon performs in cities and towns across the country. We may be appalled to think that we live in a world where we might *need* video dating, but my feeling is that it's the impersonality of our world that enrages us more than video dating or the other matchmaking services in themselves.

One of the people I interviewed in New York said that she didn't go to singles' bars per se but stopped now and then at a neighborhood bar called Tarragon's for drinks with her friends. The implication was that Tarragon's is a singles' bar, and the reason her comment stuck with me is that Tarragon's is also in my neighborhood and that I, too, stop there from time to time with friends for a couple of drinks. Yet I've never for a moment thought of it as a singles' bar. I've never tried to get picked up there, nor has anyone at Tarragon's tried to pick me up. It's a friendly enough place, though, and now that I think about it I've no doubt exchanged a few words with or smiled vaguely at a familiar face, but that's hardly the act of a desperate single.

Like attracts like as it always has, and it makes sense that a bunch of unmatched people who feel like having an occasional glass of wine or a chef's salad will be drawn to a place where the atmosphere, price and fellow customers suit them. Where else are we all supposed to go— to the closest lemonade stand? The so-called singles' bars are not really so different from the earlier soda shops, then, and computer dating, like the practice of blind dates, is just another way of bringing the old *shadchan* tradition up to date.

I suspect there's probably far less sex after an evening at a bar, or a week at a resort, Mr. Goodbar notwithstanding, than everyone thinks. I also think that few people would go through all the rigamarole, not to mention expense, of signing up for a computer date simply to find a one-time sex partner. Another one of our "new," high-tech courting institutions, the personal ads that appear in many newspapers and magazines, is in fact as old as the hills; personals date from the 1700s. One young girl I talked to did go to local bars, was open to meeting people there and described exactly what people hope to find when they experiment with new ways of meeting people. She told me: "No, I don't want to get picked up. I just want to meet somebody who maybe I'll like."

Even without statistics to back up these instincts, I feel safe in saying that most people who are single—I wish there were another word for single, as if to be single implies being incomplete—don't live their lives in the mythical fast lane. We don't all go running from disco to bar to orgies and one-night stands. Most of us live lives like any other people: We go out or stay in; We see friends for dinner or go to parties; We plan our weekends; We go on trips; We tend to the details of our lives. We're even a part of the same species as men and women who *aren't* single.

It's through these arrangements of everyday life, I think, that most courtship comes about. The coincidental meeting of a friend of a friend of a friend at a party where you thought you wouldn't know anybody; the man who lives down the hall who jogs every morning before work at the same time you do, and who leaves a note under your door one morning when you don't show up and he's worried you might be sick; a fellow student in your Russian class; someone of like spirit who shows up at a committee or campaign meeting. Relying as we do on these fortuitous occasions is a little haphazard, not to say scary; this is why it may in fact seem that you never meet anybody: There's so little structure to courtship. It's all so unpredictable. Still, and at the risk of sounding Pollyanna-ish, new faces do turn up, and most of us have been in and out of love more times and with more intensity than our ancestors could ever have hoped to be.

So, despite odds that seem stacked unfairly against us, we do manage to meet this "one true love" and that one; and each time we chart a course of love that is at once new and unexpected, and reminiscent of the times that came before....

Chapter Four

Overtures

THESE NEXT two chapters are about what happens in a romance before you get to the sex. An odd subject; we almost never, these days, think about relationships and how they work without thinking at the same time about sex. Like children who have been told they'll get dessert as soon as they finish their Brussels sprouts and who slump in their chairs until the ice cream finally comes, we tend in our love affairs to save our real attention and energies for the good stuff. What happens out of the bedroom, however, is at least as important as what happens in it: Think of the preliminaries as the Brussels sprouts of courtship. Dessert comes along in due course.

Years ago, a lot of thought and planning went into the ritual of dating, the assumption being that if everything else went right, so, when the time came, would sex. Now, we arrange a date, slap on a little deodorant and hope for the best, often devoting less care to the event than we might, for example, to preparing for a job interview.

The joys of sex are by now second nature. Everyone is supposed to know how to do it right. But that's skipping Basic Courtship 101: You have to know first that it's bad manners to bore your date with the squalid details of your last affair, or to exclaim in horror, when you get the check, at what inflation has done to the price of a hamburger.

It's easier to face any social situation once you've mastered the rules (don't eat your peas with a knife, elbows off the table, eat with the outside fork), but when it comes to dating most of us never know quite what to expect, what "surprises" might erupt. Thus you're likely to think of going out as an ordeal or, if you're thinskinned, a real trauma. So it should be good news to know that if you believe in, practice and expect good manners during the early stages of courtship you're much less likely to find it necessary to excuse yourself to go to the restroom and head instead for the parking lot to escape a bad situation.

A friend of mine tells a typical first-date horror story that good manners could have prevented. "This guy was my friend's neighbor; I met him at her house. I liked him. I was excited that he asked me out. He seemed kind of preppy so I got all prepped out, crew-neck sweater, the whole thing. Dinner was fine, then we went back to his apartment to listen to music. At about nine-thirty I went into the bathroom. I guess he thought I was putting in my diaphragm or something, but when I came out he had unfolded his convertible sofa. His shirt was unbuttoned. I felt horrible. Did he think I was so blind or so desperate that I'd just jump into bed with him? Did he think I was going to come out of the bathroom naked? I didn't even know him." She *might* have slept with him at some point, she thought, "But I wouldn't sleep with anyone who acted as crudely as that."

The question of sex, while it's the most obvious, isn't the only one to arise early on. One man I know was puzzled and angry when a woman asked him on their first date for money to pay her babysitter. "She told me that the last guy she went out with used to pay the babysitter, and I told her she should probably think seriously about going with him." A woman just out of college wondered, after accepting a date with a man she'd met at a party, just what was meant by a "date": "People keep saying to me, 'Oh, I hear you're dating Stephen,' and we hadn't even gone out yet. How could he say I was 'dating' him?"

There's a different first-date story for every first date, and many of us have had more of them than we care to think about. Offhand as we may pretend to be about them ("Oh, yeah, I'm having dinner with this guy tonight"), first dates can summon up the same sensations most of us feel before sleeping with someone for the first time: shyness, perhaps, along with excitement, fear, uncertainty and nervousness and so on. Somehow we have a "rule" that tells us it's fine, even respectable, to feel nervous when a friendship turns into a love affair, but we don't make the same allowance for first-date jitters. We're supposed to be too mature and sophisticated, too cool, for that. One assumes that just as you're supposed to outgrow acne, you're also supposed to outgrow feeling ill-at-ease over a first date, an occasion that, as everyone knows, might turn out to be the most important evening of your life.

"Brief Encounter," which used to be called "*Esquire* Goes on a Date," is a regular feature of the magazine, in which a reporter goes on a "date" with a beautiful woman, usually of the movie-star variety. Sometimes he spends the evening with her at her house in Malibu; other times they go out for an expense-account night on the town in New York. Whatever, the dates are unlike any I've ever known. Neither the reporter nor his date ever falters, even for a moment. There's never any question of what to talk about next or how to cover up if you find you've said the wrong thing, of sexual advances, of whether to hide a messy apartment. There's no need to decide whether to meet at the restaurant or go there separately, no problem about anyone's being late or dressed inappropriately or leaving home without an American Express card. Date and reporter have a glorious time and the occasion sounds just splendid in print. Fine for *Esquire*.

As for the rest of us, no matter how many sexual positions we might have memorized, despite B.A.s in Liberal Arts and familiarity with the latest movies and best sellers, regardless of age or current weight, we, the victims of broken hearts and broken marriages and numerous false starts, often step into such new situations covering our dread with the appearance of indifference. Or at best, with a wait-and-see guardedness.

For the woman, the pre-date internal monologue might go something like this: "Why didn't he tell me where we're going so that I'd know what to wear? I wish I'd had time to wash my hair. Maybe *I* was supposed to pick the place to eat, or maybe I'm supposed to eat before he comes. What if he tries to sleep with me—will he think I'm a prude if I say no? If I say yes, what will he think? What if he doesn't try to sleep with me? Maybe I should have lost weight. What happens if I like him, I really don't have time for a relationship anyway, remember what happened last time? Why did he ask me out in the first place? Why did I say yes? I wish I were staying home to watch TV; he's making me miss part forty-six of the Dr. Seuss special."

On the other side of town her date, shaving morosely, has worries of his own. "Is she used to fancy places? Should I get dressed up? Will she notice that I've only had half of my hair transplants? Does she know we're going to dinner, what if she's already eaten? Maybe I'd better eat first, too. What if she tries to pay? Or what if she's made a reservation somewhere and I don't have enough money? Should I try to sleep with her? What if I don't, will she think I'm weird? What happens if I like her, I really don't have time for a relationship anyway, remember what happened last time? Why did I ask her out in the first place? Why did she say yes? I wish I were staying home to watch TV; she's making me miss part forty-six of the Dr. Seuss special."

By the time you get this far, when you reach this all-too-familiar point where you'd rather be anyone else, anywhere else and about to do anything else, it's too late to back out. You're already immersed in the rituals of courtship. You've met, flirted, admitted to a romantic possibility, taken the first steps. Feelings are already at stake, and the occasion deserves a certain amount of ceremony.

Most other species hold to rigid and unchanging courtship etiquette. The flash of fireflies, for instance, is a coded mating signal; the male firefly flashes at the female. Each subspecies of lizard has its own specific nodding pattern: The guy nods to the lady lizard in a certain way and if she's the right kind of lizard and if she's interested, then it's her nod, so to speak. The male hermit crab has one claw larger and more gaudily colored than the other with which he waves at female hermit crabs, in a way not unlike some human males I've seen. These species have managed perfectly well for centuries, flashing and nodding and waving. In humbling contrast, we can't seem to get it together to decide which mating signals work best for us. We've been so busy taming our instincts in such matters (the process is called civilization) since the days of the cavepersons, that by now we don't even "court" anymore: We search for meaningful relationships, as we might search for a missing button.

Love brings responsibilities, but early in courtship all we have to depend upon, all that draws us together, is the fragile bond of a shared etiquette, that and the curiosity about each other that drew us together in the first place. Etiquette, oddly enough, works much like the kind of popular psychology that's practiced and studied today. People generally enter into therapy, or read up on self-improvement in how-to books, to make themselves feel better, and in turn to improve their relations with the outside world. Etiquette's similar but takes the opposite approach, suggesting that if we behave in a way that makes others feel comfortable and good we will make ourselves feel better, too—and thus improve our relations with the world. If you can go along with these admittedly imprecise definitions, a display of good manners is tantamount to a really good session with a shrink. A surprise thank-you note for a small, forgotten kindness or, in courtship, a bouquet of flowers to celebrate the occasion when you become lovers, can not only change your day but can make you feel benevolent toward the world at large.

I grew up in the do-your-own-thing era, and the ethic stretched all the way to love. The self-help, be-your-own-best-friend message for assessing love, sex and relationships was simple: Make sure your friend or spouse makes you happy and fills your needs. Not a word about manners. Not a word about behaving so that you're *both* happy and everyone's needs are filled, so far as they can be. Needless to say, courtship and marriage have never before been such a mess.

Understandably, and with apologies to my friends, I've grown obsessive about manners as I've written this book, and am now convinced that in any number of cases we excuse bad manners or write them off in some way, explaining that so-and-so's screwed up or that someone else has psychological problems. Where courtship is concerned, a faulty psyche is no excuse for bad manners—unless, of course, you're really a nut, in which case you'd better buy another book.

Gail, the roommate of an acquaintance of mine, agreed to be interviewed, and as we were talking in her apartment she began to tell me about the man she had been seeing for the past few months. We'll call him Dudley, Dud for short. The two were lovers and spent a couple of nights a week together. Their unspoken agreement was that he would call every few days, to make plans or just to check in and say hello. "I felt funny about calling him," she said. "He traveled a lot, and had to go out a lot for business dinners. So I usually waited for him to call me."

For a few weeks before I met her, she had been waiting and waiting for Dud to call. It had been nearly a month. "I probably would have called him just before this," she thought, "just to see what had happened, but there was a holiday weekend in there and I didn't want him to think I had nothing to do. After that it seemed too late to call."

All I could think of to say about him was: "Bad manners." There was more, of course. He was cruel, inconsiderate, disrespectful, small and cowardly. "Oh, no," she disagreed, "he's just...I mean...he's got all these problems. He's had a hard time with women, he had a painful divorce, he's afraid to get involved." And so on—we all know the lines. Still, I fail to see why even if someone can't, for whatever reasons, form a real attachment, he or she can't say goodbye with a show of decency.

But I'm putting the cart before the horse. You can't

break up before you've gone out, although it would save a lot of trouble in some cases if you could. The manners of courtship really begin with flirting, our counterpart to the flashing, waving and nodding noted earlier.

In its earliest definition, a flirt was a "smart blow or tap," strong enough in any case to draw attention to the striker. Naturally, what we mean by flirting changes with the times. If you're going to flirt effectively, you'll want to do it in the current fashion. We're too old to pull on each other's pigtails.

During the days of the American Puritans, a man would flirt by seizing a woman's gloves and demanding a kiss. This worked only if he didn't get caught—the fine for "unauthorized wooing" was a pound a week. The way we flirt is much closer to what was called "quizzing" in nineteenth-century England. Quizzing was just what it sounds like: a back-and-forth teasing repartee between men and women. Because quizzing hit London salons toward the end of the Victorian age, when men and women were just beginning to relax again, flirting skills were a bit rusty and it was felt that one could get better with practice. Part of flirting *is* practice—the rest is just instinct and good taste.

There are as many styles of flirting as there are flirters, but the point of flirting is always to show interest in someone, to flatter with attention while giving him or her as little proof as possible that you're doing so, and trying, at the same time, to make yourself as invulnerable as you can to being misunderstood. As a female accountant from Virginia told me, flirting is "more a certain energy than a behavior. I guess I smile and laugh, lots of eye contact and maybe a casual touch on the arm or shoulder."

Another woman, a writer, says, "I laugh at things that

aren't funny and pretend to be interested in things that are boring." From a man, an artist: "I pay close attention, present a façade of enormous intelligence, wit, compassion—it's showing off without seeming a braggart or an obnoxious ass." Others cite "nervous humor," a demeanor that's "even more sarcastic than usual." Now and then a woman resorts to a "soft, wistful and demure approach." One man, who signed his questionnaire Englebert Humperdinck, although I recognize his handwriting, flirts or claims to by making use of "socks filled with rolls of quarters."

We are, as a rule, somber and analytical, sometimes too much so, about courtship, but it's a mistake to flirt with a heavy hand. You don't flirt to get somewhere; if you're flirting you're already there. Flirting is something to do for its own sake. If you want the flirtation to lead in another direction, you'll have to change your tone and manner. People who go to a party hoping to "meet someone" (and why else would you go to a party? If you didn't want to meet people you'd stay home) tend to flirt with some desperation, pleading more than flirting. That won't work. If a friendship comes of a flirtation, it will seem to have come on its own.

The charm of flirting is that you can practice with just about anyone you know. Children quickly learn the value of flirting with their parents; married people flirt, sometimes even with each other. Most of us flirt with our dentists in the futile hope that if we do the drilling won't hurt as much (dentists, you'll notice, don't flirt back). Harmless office flirtations can be carried on for years without ever crossing the line into romance or sex. The rules for flirtations of this sort are the same as for those you hope might lead to something more.

Flirting is not the time to share your life story, for example. First of all, you'll have nothing to talk about the next time you meet (and if your life story is as dull as most life stories are, you might not even get a second chance). Moreover, if you do you will probably end up feeling that you've told too much, with that regretful anxiety that comes from confiding in relative strangers. Intimacies are for intimates.

It's also a bad idea to tell other people's life stories. You never know who knows whom, and gossip, newsworthy and convenient as it can be, is not something to divulge until you know where the divulgee's loyalties lie. Anyway, gossip is not a very good way of showing yourself in the best light.

What you do talk about—despite the prevailing idea today that conversations don't count unless they're "heavy"—are matters of absolutely no importance. Like crazy inventions and landlords and how silly hula hoops seem now. I've always admired people who can come up with such lines as, "This is the kind of day that reminds me of a frog-shaped kite I had when I was a kid," which could lead to more talk about kites, other pleasures and maybe going kite-flying next Saturday afternoon. It's a good idea to have a few such lines for every occasion stored away in the back of your mind, especially if the brightest thing you've ever found to say at a cocktail party is, "Hey, that's an interesting looking vodka-and-tonic you have there. I mean you've got a slice of lime and not a wedge."

Prim as it sounds, sexual innuendo and references to certain parts of the anatomy are also out of place in flirtation. Reasons of taste aside, flirtation is subtle and delicate, like sneaking up on a butterfly, and you don't want your audience to know what you have in mind.

As a case in point, a young woman I talked to was embarrassed when a teasing conversation accidentally turned sour. "He was talking about things he was good at, like fixing stuff and crossword puzzles and his work. We were kidding around and having a good time, and I was thinking that I wanted him to ask me out. I wanted to keep the conversation going and I couldn't think what to say next, so I asked him if he was also good in bed. I meant it to be funny, but it sounded so blatant, cheap. After that I felt awful, he did, too, and the whole thing fell apart. It wasn't like me to say that. I was trying too hard. I didn't even want to go out with him anymore by then; I just wanted to get away."

Flirting can also be dangerous when it gets hard-edged. A friendly challenge ("I dare you to jump in the pool") is one thing, but it's confusing and disconcerting to try to get more than one message across. Crossed signals are self-defeating. A newly divorced friend of mine, an attractive and very funny man of about forty, was confiding his social troubles to me one night over drinks. He began by saying that he "didn't understand women anymore," following that train of thought awhile before he got to the point. His specific complaint was about a woman he knew through his work and wanted to know better. "It's complicated," he said. "Sometimes I think she's interested, too, but then we'll start talking and I feel as if she's, I don't know, almost making fun of me. She acts as if she knows something about me; she's aggressive in a strange way. I'd be afraid to ask her out." This woman's *modus operandi*—assuming my friend had the thing figured out correctly and she really was interested—was obviously not helping her cause.

It never works to pretend to be more sophisticated than you really are, and a little nervousness between strangers is not only perfectly natural, it can also be disarming. It's more important to create an aura of attentiveness while you're flirting than it is to try to be witty; an inane comment here and there—remember Annie Hall?

and her friend Woody Allen?—can hold you until you think of the right thing to say or do next.

Turning a flirtation into an invitation is something else again. For this you really have to have your wits about you. And even the question of who asks whom isn't so simple as it once was.

I've always envied men what seemed to me the unfair advantage of being able to suggest a date, to say, "Can I see you again?" "Can I call you?" "Would you like to have dinner?" Not being able to do that, as I for one am not, is a real handicap. I never thought much about the fact that men might feel anxious or paralyzed at the thought of asking for a date, or that they might regard the set-up as a burden, but of course men do have qualms about it. As James Thurber wrote:

> We all know, I think, that nature gave man whiskers and a mustache with the quaint idea in mind that these would prove attractive to the female. We all know that, far from attracting her, whiskers only made her nervous and gloomy, so that man had to go in for somersaults, tilting with lances, and performing feats of parlor magic to win her attention; he also had to bring her candy, flowers, and the furs of animals. It is common knowledge that in spite of all these "love displays" the male is constantly being turned down, insulted, or thrown out of the house.

Hard as it may be for a man to ask a woman out, it is infinitely harder in my (biased) opinion, for a woman to go first. In *Playboy*'s "Dear Playmate" column half a dozen bunny "panelists" take turns each month answering what are essentially questions of romantic etiquette. One month the question was: "Can you ask a man out? If so, how do you do it?" Of the women questioned, only one (and these are *bunnies*, remember) admitted that she could ask a man out directly. The rest described more serpentine strategies of luring a man into asking them out first, and admitted to shyness, the fear of rejection and the need, for age-old reasons of pride, to make the strategy appear anything but obvious.

What is noteworthy here is that the question of whether women may do the asking has at least made the pages of such an austere publication as *Playboy*. Maybe this means it's just barely possible that one day soon women will feel free to ask men out without worrying about it any more than men do now. Noteworthy as that may be, it's still not much help. While the men and women I talked to agree in principle that women should have equal asking rights, it's true that many women are afraid to ask and many men are put off by being asked. So even though Sam may fervently argue that Seducia has every right to ask him out, if she were actually to call up with a rousing, "Hey, Sam, you free on Friday?" he might well run home to his mother for a supper of macaroni and cheese—even if he's fifty years old.

Nevertheless, the problem of supply and demand being what it is, women have a responsibility to the species to help courtship along, and it's well within the bounds of good manners—and romantic tradition—to do so. Once upon a time, women resorted to their wiles (sounds like a disease, doesn't it—women's wiles) to get men to ask them out. Men, with their access to the direct approach, never had to cultivate wiles of their own. Wiles were subtle means of cornering men, often with the aid of aunts and cousins and friends, so that the poor man was forced, by the weight of odds and numbers, to cave in, or as the old folk saying goes: A man chases a girl until she catches him. By the 1940s, however, etiquette writers could see that times were tough; wiles weren't enough. A young girl interested in a young man was advised to confront him head-on: "Mother and I will be home Thursday evening. I should like to have you meet her." That sounds more like a threat than an invitation to me; nowadays we try to be more creative about it. What's more, women don't have wiles these days—instead, they have assertiveness.

Most of the women I talked to or heard from when I was writing this book—once they thought about it— admitted that they'd invented ingenious ways to set dates in motion, even if they fell short of actually being able to ask. The etiquette here seems to be: Good manners permit making it clear to the man that you're willing to be asked out, and making it as easy as possible for him to ask you—making it, in fact, easier for him to do so than not to.

A New York woman, for example, who casts commercials for television, has often called men she's met to suggest that they might be perfect for the commercial she happens to be working on ("One time it backfired, though; I had to put him through a screen test and he never even asked me out."). Another woman, from Minneapolis, will call men to see if they are willing to test new products for her market-research firm. In the book publishing business it's commonplace for single women to send books to acquaintances, chosen with their interests in mind, and every time a book goes out a thank you—maybe even a date—comes back. Your job won't do you much good in this respect if you're in the athlete's-foot powder business, of course, which means that some women will have to use their imaginations. But this isn't all bad. "I'd been waiting six years for this guy to ask me out," a woman from Kansas City visiting a friend of mine told me. I asked her how the date had come about finally, and she said, "Oh, he doesn't even know my name. What happened was that I met a friend of his, and got *him* to arrange a blind date." A suburban divorcée from Detroit, using, as she describes it, "all the courage I could muster," once called a man she knew to find out how to join his ski club. He enthusiastically invited her to come along with him sometime; the only drawback, as far as she could tell, was that she then had to take up skiing.

For many women, especially fairly young women or women who work, suggesting lunch is different from asking for a real date. A casual restaurant, the implicit Dutch treat and the fact that lunch is "finite" make the whole affair seem innocent of secondary motives. And some prefer to rely on the mails. "I don't know, maybe it's forward," says a Los Angeles executive secretary, "but when I meet someone I always try to figure out something that interests him so that I can send him an article or an ad about it. A new movie or whatever. Then he can call and say thank you."

It's difficult, of course, for some women to take the initiative at all. But if you're one of these women, the trick is to practice being friendly and well mannered whether you're interested romantically or not: anti-shyness training, in effect. Good manners are good manners, and if they're not returned in kind, the bad manners are not yours. My friend Colleen, who is terribly shy and could never be accused of coming on to a cookie, has been taught that it's impolite to leave a party or gathering without saying goodbye to the people, women included, with whom she's spent a lot of time during the evening, and to tell them how much she enjoyed meeting them. To her surprise, she recently went up to a man to say goodbye and, although by that time he was talking with another group of people, he took her aside and said, "Oh, hi, I wanted to get your phone number before you left."

Had she simply thanked the host and bolted, as most people seem to, she would have left behind a much fainter impression.

There are many other ways for men and women to be friendly, even if shyness makes a forthright overture out of the question. Margaret Smyth, for example, makes a point of spelling her name to those she meets—"I just say, Smith's not so common if it's spelled with a 'y.'" This approach won't help if your name is Lightbulb, but I hope the point is clear: Part of the comfort of good manners is that they're wonderful to hide behind, and today directness is vital to good manners. I'm shy myself, and I find it easier to talk to people if I remind myself to be polite than I do if I try to work on my "communication skills."

It's wise to remember, too, that men are by now accustomed to courting women who are direct when it comes to romance, and who are straightforward enough to give them some kind of indication that they're interested. Women aren't supposed to be able to double as bathmats anymore. To say, "Oh, I'd like to see that exhibit, too," "Maybe I'll see you sometime at the driving range," "I hope to see you again" or some other variation is friendly, polite, encouraging—and noncommital enough to risk virtually nothing. Several of the men I've interviewed have commented that, "I would have asked her out but I didn't think she was interested." It's rude not to seem interested enough to show that you are interested, especially if you really *are* interested.

It's a poignant comment on our sense of propriety that many women are embarrassed by the assertiveness to which they nevertheless feel entitled. Recently I talked to two people who live together. Bill casually remarked that they first went out when Alice tracked him down and finally asked him for a date. "I did not," she objected with real vehemence. (I had the feeling that this was a familiar exchange.) Who tracked down whom is not terribly important, but it is important, I think, for men to be especially kind to women who take that first step. Such light mockery, even if there's no harm intended, might mean nothing in the years to come. But we're not that liberated yet, and the man who fails to respond appreciatively to a woman's advances, which is to say a man who does not treat a woman as he himself would like to be treated under similar circumstances, is despicable.

Women, too, have the responsibility to be kind when men call. No matter how long any of us has been asking people for dates it doesn't, as a male friend reminds me, get much easier. "Every time I get ready to call, and I'm thirty-five now, I'm always afraid she'll say: 'You? Go out with *you*? You've got to be kidding.'"

On my questionnaires I asked people to list pet peeves they had discovered during their various dating experiences. Most people listed the blights that happen later on, about the time your beloved misplaces his or her halo and begins to get on your nerves in a serious way. But one man mentioned a time when he got up his courage and called a woman he liked to ask her out. She had replied that she had to check her calendar, could he call her at the office the next day? He wondered what such imperiousness might have meant. Were her fingers broken, so that she couldn't call *him* the next day? Was this an excuse to say no, or was she so busy that he would never find a place in her life? He lost his nerve and never called back.

Because we don't learn our manners by rote anymore, we tend sometimes to speak in a kind of shorthand that often comes across as either rudeness or a lack of grace. I don't want to sound too etiquette book-y, but there are ways to issue and accept dates, and there are ways not to. We all like that feeling of easy confidence that comes from knowing more or less what's going on in our own lives, and as far as arranging dates is concerned, we can best achieve this by following the formalities that were developed for just that reason.

One contemporary bad habit is to invite someone out with an expansive, "Hey, let's get together next weekend. I'll call you." These words have done to manners what the chemical companies have done to our rivers. Does this mean that the person who has agreed to "get to-gether" is obliged to spend the next five days lounging by the phone? Does next weekend mean Saturday night? a date for church? tennis? a weekend trip to Paris?

When I was in high school, boys were supposed to call by Wednesday for a date on Friday, and by Thursday for a Saturday night date. (I haven't any idea whether the boys were even aware of this rule.) If the call didn't come in by the deadline, girls arranged to go to a slumber party; girls were busy if the call came late. Thankfully, this schedule went out with be-ins. It's no crime not to have a date for Saturday by Friday—and there are worse things to do than spend Saturday night at home alone. What's more, you don't even have to spend your week-ends hiding in your living room with the lights turned off on the chance that someone important might drive by and see that you're not out on the town.

Still, the promise of a date ("Let's get together") is by no means the same thing as a date. If the call doesn't come within what you decide is your time limit (allowing an extra day for the usual slovenliness), feel free to make other plans. More important, whether you're a man or a woman, make a point of making other plans, especially if the waiting is driving you crazy. Remind yourself that spur-of-the-moment invitations count only if the details are immediately forthcoming. If and when the offender does call, and such calls sometimes come weeks or marriages later, treat the call as if it were the first invitation. You're off to a bad start if you're angry or defensive from the beginning, and a good way to avoid bad feelings is to distinguish between an "I'll call you" and a genuine invitation.

"Do you want to hang out on Friday?" is another way not to issue an invitation. Nor is, "Do you want to do something on Friday?" A proper invitation—and this really isn't so difficult—zeroes in on the specifics. "Would you like to have dinner on Friday? I thought we might go to the new gourmet goulash place." Most people really do appreciate knowing ahead of time what they'll be doing, what they should plan to wear, when they're expected to turn up. If you don't know exactly where you'll be going, you should still try to give at least a clue as to whether jeans will or will not do. If you really do plan to hang out, say what you mean by that.

If there's a movie or some other entertainment involved, you get two points for asking first whether it would amuse your date. Should you start out by saying how you love to smoke dope and go to old Disney films, you won't give your would-be date much of a chance to say politely that he or she saw *Bambi* at age five, and that once was enough. You get another two points for supplying the estimated time of departure when you first call. There's nothing worse than being ready for a dinner date at 6:45 only to have your date call at 7:00 to say the reservation's for 9:00. (Actually, there are worse things, but it's a nice touch to go for broke and do the whole thing right.)

The recipient of the invitation also has a few things to remember—this sounds fundamental, I know, but you have to start somewhere before you work up to dimming the lights. Contemporary shorthand won't do here, either. You don't want to leave the caller wondering whether you really want to go to the grand opening of the new car wash or whether you accepted because you were caught off guard. There's a world of difference (again, the difference is manners) between saying, "Okay, that'd be fine," and saying, "Oh, I'd really like to do that; I'm glad you called." Accepting an invitation gracefully is not the same as accepting gratefully. You're not, after all, saying, "Oh, I'm so happy you called. I haven't had a date in three years."

If the person asking you out decides, for whatever private reasons, to keep the nature of the date a secret, don't be reticent about asking in a general way what you'll be doing. You can pinpoint "we'll go somewhere" by saying something like, "Oh, what would be fun to do?" It keeps the conversation going and it helps people who need a little direction.

It's also acceptable to make final plans on the morning of the date, so long as you both have had a general idea from the first what to expect. ("Great. We'll have dinner on Monday, seven-thirty, eight. I'll call you that morning.")

A number of men have asked me what to do about women who call with a specific invitation—"I've been given passes to a debate between two anthropologists on transcultural bathing habits"—and whether they are required to follow their "no" with an invitation in return. Slightly startled by women who so boldly take the lead, some men feel that vestiges of chivalry require them to ask a woman who calls first out, at least once. Nonsense. This confuses chivalry with the idea of male superiority. A reluctant man is as uninspiring as a reluctant woman, and neither has an obligation to return an invitation. Neither does a woman have the right to make a man who refuses a date feel like a boor by bursting out crying on the phone, for example, or hanging up and saying, "All right for you, Malcolm!" Nor should she switch in midstream to old-fashioned girl: "Well, if you can't make it, do you promise you'll call me up soon?"

There are plenty of gentle ways to turn down an invitation. Remarks like, "Ick, the very thought of you makes me want to throw up," could eventually bring down our entire culture. If you think a date to go snowshoveling sounds dull, or if you have other plans for the next snowfall, the ball's in your court when you refuse. If you'd like to make a date for another time say so: "My shovel's in the shop now, but I'd love to, another time." You might add, "The long-range forecast calls for snow next Thursday. Could you do it then?" It's a little unfair to expect the caller to think up two invitations in one call.

If you don't want to go, ever, it's decent to say so as soon as you can to save having to do so later. In the interest of being kind or lazy, many people thank the caller and leave the question of the future ambiguous, leading to more calls and more vague refusals. Better to say, "What a good idea, but I'm kind of tied up for a few weeks (months?) and it would probably be better if I didn't." Or, "That's really nice, but I'm seeing someone now and it would be best if I didn't." I once tried the latter (it was true), and I had to laugh when the man said he would try again, if he were still free, in six months. Circumstances change, and you may decide it's not unfair or disloyal to whomever you're seeing now to leave a few doors ajar, or to strike up a new friendship, but out of consideration for the newcomer make it absolutely clear that that's what you're doing.

Courtship thus begins long before we really think of it as such. The bespectacled, solemn little second-grade boy who is given a microscope will inevitably, upon seeing his first planarian through the lens, decide he wants to be a scientist. Years later, if he does indeed become a scientist, his parents will point with affection and pride to that moment, recalling how something in the boy's consciousness lit up and how that something never faltered. If somewhere along the way somebody had made fun of the kid's microscope, then his dream of being a scientist might have been shattered, and the kid would remember his erstwhile goal only many years later and in his shrink's office. Courtship works the same way. When it comes to our feelings we are like children. To understand courtship is to understand that these feelings need to be nurtured at every turn, and that we invest something of ourselves with every move we make.

Page after page, and still we're not much beyond the flashing, nodding and waving noted earlier. For fireflies, lizards and hermit crabs it would be time now to carry out the responsibility to their species, but we human beings take courtship rituals much more seriously. Sex is still a full chapter away. Probably a good thing, too, because as Bertrand Russell defined it, courtship works as "nature's safeguard against sexual fatigue."

Chapter Five

Time-Sharing

MY FRIENDS and I have long distinguished between a Date and a Date Date. A simple Date is the most conventional occasion you'll find in contemporary courtship. You're relative strangers, and you'll behave in a relatively formal way. You might have met once or twice before— at a party, through some friends, as a result of your job or some interest you have in common—and somehow that meeting has turned into this date. Your first impression was pleasing, or at least not a disaster. You feel you've got everything to gain or, at worst, little to lose.

A Date Date, however, is an event. You're going out with someone you already think you like. Your hope, although you haven't voiced it except to yourself (and possibly your eleven closest confidantes), is that this might turn into something. You don't dare say what. The two of you already have a history together. Perhaps you've long been friends or acquaintances; perhaps you once knew each other and recently have met again after years and many changes in your lives. You're pretty certain that the attraction's mutual. And you feel as if you're about sixteen years old, and that this is your first date ever.

The third kind of date, which a man I interviewed referred to as an "um, unexpected pleasure," is the kind that makes ancestors turn in their graves, although many of us have learned to handle such occasions with aplomb. These are the evenings when you start off somewhere and end up, to your surprise, somewhere else, with someone you never planned to be with that night. (This is not the same, even if you should end up sleeping together, as a one-night stand, which, by definition, has nothing to do with courtship. The etiquette for a one-night stand? Safety first, manners second and beware especially of sexually transmitted diseases.) A date in the unexpected-pleasure category involves two well-meaning friends or acquaintances who happen to get together in the most casual way and who let the evening set its own rules. "You're going uptown, too? Want to walk together for awhile, then we could share a cab?" "It's too crowded here. Do you want to go somewhere for a drink?" As for manners, one does one's best on short notice. The next date will really count as your first and you'll probably feel more shy then, since you'll be wondering what it was about Bertha or Ivan that made the first evening so magical. (If you count blind dates as dates, they're covered in Chapter Nine.)

A recent rock song advises taking courtship "step by step," and says the man's first step is to "ask her out and treat her like a lady." An etiquette book published in 1873 is stricter about the gentleman's responsibility in the first stage:

> We urge him, before he ventures to take any step towards the pursuit of this object to consider well his position and prospects in life, and reflect whether they are such as to justify him deliberately seeking to win the young lady's affections, with the view of making her his wife at no distant period.

And the lady's:

> First let us hope that the inclination is mutual; at all events, that the lady views her admirer with preference, that she deems him not unworthy of her favorable regard, and that his attentions are agreeable to her.

Courtship's no joke when you have to assess your prospects for marriage before you so much as have a beer together. But even today, though we may not always admit it, most of us don't ask for or accept a date without putting a favorite happily-ever-after romantic fantasy on "re-wind" and playing it through again.

On the first date we're in an odd position. On the one hand, we all know that courtship is supposed to lead somewhere; that's built into our genes. On the other hand, because we're cool and liberated, and because we've all been knocked around some, we know, too, that such expectations and a subway token will get you to Brooklyn. So even though *you* know you're going on the date because you hope to fall in love, you have to pretend, as we all do, that you're going with nothing more in mind than the evening ahead. The last thing you'd ever say aloud on a first date is the question that's really on your mind: "Hey, what do you think? Will we fall in love or not?"

In previous generations, when everyone assumed that sooner or later marriage was inevitable, men and women took special care with first dates...just in case this time it was for real. Now that we've discarded that assumption, or pretend to, I've noticed that many of us try to act as mysterious as possible about our intentions—that way, no one will ever know what you're hoping will happen. No one will ever be able to accuse you of having the wrong ideas or, for that matter, any clear ideas at all about what you want. Often what this means is that we behave on a date so as to suggest that the date means nothing or, in other words, we end up working very hard to perfect atrocious manners. When Dustin Hoffman took Katherine Ross to the striptease bar in *The Graduate*, for example, he was telling her to expect very little from him: Bad manners can be a vicious way to say painful things.

Granted, the circumstances were a bit extraordinary (Hoffman was, after all, sleeping with Katherine Ross's mother). But the fact remains that many people become social stuntpersons on dates, so that one's date is forced to go home later and wonder, "What was he (or she) all about?" or worse, "What's wrong with *me*?" Whether these extremes of self-protectivism should be discussed in a psychology textbook or an etiquette book is irrelevant. If you're going to make your companion feel weird you shouldn't go out in the first place.

The first "rule" for happy dating, then, is to acknowledge, at least to yourself, that you're available and hope to be interested; that is, after all, why you're there in the first place. A second rule, or maybe a footnote to the first rule, is that if your date doesn't know that you're married, gay, living with someone, attached to someone, an escaped convict or incapable of being civil once you've slept with someone new, you're taking cruel risks with other people's hearts. Unlike golf, courtship can't be played with handicaps. If only a century ago one had to think about marriage before honorably going on a date, the least we can do today is to tell the truth about our personal arrangements.

The most sincere compliment you can offer your date is to show up on time, clean, energetic, expectant and sober. This is schoolmarm talk (I kept trying to leave this paragraph out, but in good conscience couldn't), but I've had dismal experiences, and so have others I've talked to, with people who call just when the date's supposed to begin only to give you a progress report on where they are at the moment and all the things they have to do before they'll be able to make it. Or with those who arrive looking as if they'd spent the afternoon mud-wrestling, or after a "few" drinks with some "old friends" (these last are likely to come and pick you up to take you back to the bar where their friends, still drinking, are saving seats for the two of you). Or even with someone who has just finished a knock-down fight with an ex-lover or spouse and somehow thinks you'll enjoy spending the evening listening to an account of the battle. You request or accept a date in good faith, and it's better to cancel the whole thing, rude as that may be, if you can't carry it out in the same spirit.

You're also accountable for seeing to it, as well as you can, that your date has a good time. We've come to believe that dates just "evolve" or "happen"; they don't. Dates require effort and energy on both parts. What's more (and this part may not seem too fair), if things do happen to work out, you'll both have to work a lot harder later.

At a flea market a while back I found a book called *Phunology*, which was published with great success about sixty years ago. *Phunology* lists hundreds of getting-to-know-you games for young men and women, and I thought it might suggest some amusing first-date ideas for today—but the games it proposes make Spin the Bottle sound pornographic: "It would be lots of fun to serve ice cream to couples and have them eat from his or her saucer [sic] with spoons that are tied together with a string nine inches long." By suggesting that dates should be planned, I don't mean that they be overplanned, in the spirit of phunology. The aim here is to work hard to achieve the natural look.

Even if you have your very own Pac-Man game, don't plan to spend the first couple of dates at home. It's easier to become acquainted on neutral territory, and there are fewer possible distractions (ringing phones, wandering cockroaches, neighbors taking singing lessons) if you're out and able to give your undivided attention to your companion.

"It turned out that the movie we wanted to see had already left town, and neither of us was hungry yet, so we went over to his house to have a drink and figure out what to do," said Pamela, describing an evening where she ended up at her date's house, "chez Marc." "His roommate was supposed to be out but he came home early, with his girl friend and some other people. They brought more wine, so we all sat around for awhile, then someone ordered a pizza. I liked Marc, but I started to feel really out of it—everyone there knew each other and nobody was really talking to me. We never went to the movie or out to dinner, and I began to feel really closed in and out of place. Finally, about one o'clock, I just went home." As it happened, Pamela and Marc went out for several months after that evening, but she still remembers how uncomfortable she felt that first night as a loner among his friends. Similarly, a person who gets dragged to a party where he or she doesn't know anyone (including his or her date) is likely to feel equally stranded.

As another approach, both men and women—particularly women—will often initiate dates when they "happen" to have "these tickets," but unless you need the ruse of tickets to go through with the invitation in the first place, the ticket approach might not be the best one either. (And never "happen" to have tickets unless you really do have them. After inviting a man she liked to a limited-engagement something or other, a woman I know found to her embarrassment that there wasn't a ticket within miles, and to save face she had to invent a stolen pocketbook at the last minute.)

The problem with theater dates at this stage of a romance is obvious: You'll never figure out, unless you talk your way through an evening, whether you have anything to talk about in the first place. My feeling is that you might as well get this hard part over with as soon as you can. There's a theory that a movie, followed by dinner, over which, if all else fails, you can always talk about the movie, makes for a pretty good date—and it can. But at a movie your foot will fall asleep, you'll have nowhere to put your knees and elbows, and you'll have to say "excuse me" practically every time you breathe. Unless you're pretty close to begin with (in which case you'll sit through the entire thing thinking about how attracted you are to the person next to you, and you'll miss the point of the movie or play anyway), you might be better off skipping such entertainment the first time around.

The temptation at this point, I know, is to whine that there's nothing left to do—but, of course, as any etiquette-book writer will tell you, that's ridiculous. Without lapsing into phunology, the two of you can walk around a museum, a gallery or an exhibition of shoelace art together. You can do something sporty. (Once I had a date to go swimming in an indoor pool. In the locker room I took out my contact lenses so that the chlorine wouldn't irritate my eyes, figuring that my date would find me stumbling around by the pool. But he took his contact lenses out, too. Because the pool was large and crowded, it was close to an hour before we finally bumped into each other; by then we both half-assumed that we'd been deserted.) Or you can go to a club to listen to music. Most often you'll have dinner.

In this case the restaurant should be no problem; almost any place not currently in violation of the health code will do. There are those who think the first time calls for a place a cut above the ordinary, but I disagree; if you insist on the most expensive or glamorous place in town you'll be broke by the time you come across your one true love. Think it through, though, and choose or suggest a place where you can both feel comfortable, where your eardrums won't be threatened by the music, where your friends won't be heckling you from the next table and where the atmosphere is cozy and fun without being intimidating. And remember the old rule that whoever is being treated should not order the most expensive item on the menu (if you're not certain at this point where the check is going to end up, all the more reason to keep away from stuff like Surf 'n Turf).

Most people I've talked to still feel that, if he can, the man should pick the woman up at her home, even (oddly enough) if she's the one who has asked him out. As with so many of our so-called "customs" today, this one's not cast in stone, and often it's simply more convenient to meet at, let's say, the restaurant. A woman with children might prefer that her kids not meet every man she goes out with; another woman might have a roommate who teaches a shiatsu class in the living room on Tuesdays. Similarly, a man might have a frantic schedule and find it difficult to get to another part of town in addition to doing everything else he has to do. Some women would rather take their own cars, to be sure that they can end the date whenever they want and drive themselves home.

Still, the ritual of who picks up whom, when and where,

exists, and to be impeccably polite one must acknowledge it. If a man offers to pick you up and you would rather he didn't don't say, "Um, well, I'll just meet you at the restaurant." That sounds as if you don't want him in your house. You may, in fact, not want him in your house, and that's where etiquette comes in handy. Smooth the edges of your refusal: "Oh, thank you, but that's about the time the children have supper and I hate to disrupt them. Why don't we meet at the restaurant?" If you're the man and can't for some reason pick the woman up, you should let her know that *you* know you're skipping a step. Instead of saying, "Be at Mr. Bob's Chop and Flop House at seven-thirty," you might try: "Would you mind meeting me at Hamburger Harry's at seven-thirty? I'm not sure that I'll be through with my meeting in time to pick you up."

Once you're together, don't let the worry over good manners get in the way of a good time. I talked to a divorced woman in her fifties—who found that after thirty years of marriage, dating was something like "shell shock"—who continually annoyed herself with a habit she had of giving the men she met "tests" she made up as she went along. "I know that things have changed," she said, "but I always notice the little things, like if a man doesn't open the car door." She herself concluded that this was her way of distancing herself from new men—and her way of trying to make her world orderly and predictable. Her preoccupation with doing things the "right" way, in an age when there usually isn't just one right way, intruded on her judgment of the finer points of a man's character. Etiquette is not supposed to turn people into social robots; it's enough if we can depend upon it simply to make the world a more pleasurable and comprehensible place. Yet many of us wonder which of the old-fashioned courtesies still apply and which do not.

When a man picks a woman up at her home, must she offer him a drink? Based on my informal survey, the drink is optional. So don't spend all day making carrot curlicues or melt-in-your-mouth puff pastries. You'll both feel that you have to eat them all, which could weigh down the evening considerably. It also looks a little silly if you go the other way and just set out a celery stalk. Offer a drink only if it feels like the right thing to do, and don't worry about it if he asks for anything peculiar, the definition of peculiar being anything you don't have on hand. There will be plenty of time later to stock up on that banana-flavored Scotch he always orders when you're out together.

I recently spent half an hour standing on a street corner with a friend, counting pairs of people to see how many men walked on the curbside. (Call it research if you want. Actually it was a hot night and we had nothing better to do.) Not counting men walking together arm in arm, which brought the control group down substantially, the ratio was about sixty–forty in favor of men on the curbside. So I'll agree to give up the curbside rule if you promise not to wear your portable headphones unless your friend has a set too.

Opening car doors. On getting into the car, it's a great gesture for the person holding the keys to open the passenger door first; the passenger then can unlock the driver's door from inside the car (sometimes the driver won't see what you've done, and will then re-lock the door as he or she attempts to open it—still, it's worth the try). If the doors are unlocked to begin with—although why would anyone leave car doors unlocked today?—the man need not open the door, although of course a gentleman would open the door if you were both all dressed up. On getting out of the car, a woman should *never* expect a man to run around and open her door; if she does she has no right to be angry if she's still in the car after he's finished his dinner. As for regular doors, whoever gets to it first opens it. And that, I think, is enough about doors.

I love the expression "to stand on ceremony"; I think of a real place labeled "ceremony" with a bunch of people standing on it. But don't stand there on a date. Gentlemen are no longer required to pull out chairs, light cigarettes, help with coats. I've never met one, either, who can manage an umbrella for two. But if a gentleman chooses to perform a courtesy, don't, if you're a woman, interpret it politically. When we got around to talking about courtesies and courtship, a man I interviewed recalled a woman (maybe here I should say Woman) with whom he'd spent one very long evening: "Every time I opened the door for her—it was like a Pavlovian response—she began to talk about women's lib."

One of the especially odd rules of good manners my mother taught me was that in a restaurant I should give my order to my date, who would then pass it on to the waiter. Dutifully, during my first years of courting, I tried this approach, but most of the time felt foolish talking to the man while the waiter wrote down what I was saying. And usually I compromised by talking to both, earnestly explaining to the man I was with that I would start with the oysters, then making direct eye contact with the waiter to announce: lamb chops.

The best way around this problem is to eat only in Chinese restaurants, where you can order dishes to share, and one person can do the ordering. The second-best way is for the woman to give her own order; then she'll have only herself to blame if she forgets to tell the waiter to hold the anchovies. (And don't stand on ceremony— there it is again—when it comes time to order the wine. If a man chooses Blue Nun, it might not be in the best of taste to stop him, but it's probably a good idea anyway.)

Table manners—the halfway point of a first date— should be no problem by now. If you don't know how to use chopsticks, you won't get away with pretending you do. If you don't know how to use a fork, don't go out to dinner. And this is much too early to try your companion's escargot or cheesecake without being invited to. (As an enthusiastic member of the just-a-bite school, I find this painful to admit.) Now what you have to do is think of something to talk about.

Sex and politics were once the hottest items on the list of subjects forbidden for mixed company; now they're among the most neutral. We don't have such a forbidden list anymore, but to decide whether what you want to talk about is suitable for a first date, ask yourself "Is this the subject that interests me most passionately?" If your answer is yes, stop yourself at once. You're probably headed into dangerous conversational territory.

If you suspect you're already "in like," i.e., what comes before "in love," and your friend feels the same way, you can talk about practically anything and sound absolutely scintillating; neither of you will be paying attention anyway. But if you're not quite up to that point yet, banned subjects include: your hairdresser; how badly you're treated by your boss, your ex-spouse, your ex-boy friend, girl friend or cat; your children; money or inflation; and anything you vow you'll "never do"—like get married again, have children or move out of the city. These last three items might cause a lot of confusion later, as the people who bring them up are those likeliest to get married again, have children or move to Wyoming.

My panel of distinguished experts has suggested that I include, as additional subjects *not* to talk about, nose jobs, hair-coloring or straightening, face-lifts, tummy-tucks or transplants.

While it's not exactly the most laid-back thing to do, I see nothing wrong with imagining your conversation ahead of time. One used to hear of "brilliant conversationalists"; I doubt they got to be that way by accident. These days you don't have to be one: It's enough to be able to say of someone, "He's a pretty funny guy." Often we'll protect ourselves from seeming too interested or too eager by saying that if someone doesn't like me "the way I am" that's his or her problem. Maybe, but if you study the people who strike you as gifted socially, you'll see that they're the ones who meet others halfway, or go even a little beyond that. And they don't fall into the conversational trap that the writer Fran Lebowitz describes when she writes that "the opposite of talking isn't listening; the opposite of talking is waiting."

"Third subjects," as a man I know describes it, are the things you ought to talk about when you're out with someone you don't know well. Or, as one woman, whose dates invariably turn into friendships if not romances, explains, "You sort of prepare for a date, the way you'd prepare for an exam. If you're going out with a stockbroker you check to see whether the market's up or down." This won't indicate that you're trying too hard or that you care too much, but it will show that you're interested—and interesting. Because romances are not always a matter of instant recognition between soul mates, you'll have a better time if you do stick to "third subjects," neutral topics your grandmother might have called "parlor talk." Books, movies, vacation spots, social attitudes; a little about your job and interests—with equal time for your date to talk about things that matter to him or her. A good conversationalist will invariably learn and reveal a lot just by discussing the weather. And you do have to keep talking, at least until the check comes....

When it comes time to pay the bill, most of us lean forward in our seats as if about to witness a great drama: Will she offer to pay? Will he accept, or ask her for money? Will he simply pay while she refreshes her blush-on? Will she let him? Will life go on as before?

The question of who pays the bill is, as everybody knows, loaded with the symbolism of dominance, submission, obligation, one's standing with creditors and the like. And because there are so many what-ifs connected with the issue, I've devised a chart to help explain the etiquette:

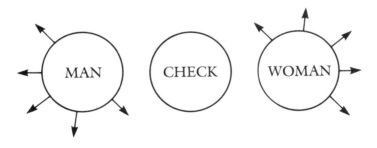

On second thought, this point may best be left un-charted. Still, there are a few questions that can be an-swered simply. The first real change is that it is never in bad taste for the woman to offer to pay her share—unless, of course, she's not sincere about the offer. Nor is it in bad taste, under most circumstances, for the man to ac-cept her offer. If the woman has invited the man out, she should expect to pay, although she can accept the offer to go Dutch.

In most cases, however, the answer is not so cut and dried. Technically, on most first dates, the woman is the man's guest; thus she should not be expected to pay, and it's not rude the first time if she fails to offer. Financial arrangements will be fine-tuned later. Nor should the man ask her for money on the first date unless he has specified ahead of time that he's planning to do so. Yet I'd agree with Karl Marx that what the issue finally comes down to is "From each according to his means." There's enough in life to get depressed about without haggling over who's going to pay for a couple of cheeseburgers.

If the man clearly has more money than the woman, he should, without question, pay this time; if he has substantially less money, she should insist on paying her half. If both have relatively equal salaries and both can afford the dinner without hardship, again the man should be the host; if both have relatively equal salaries and both salaries are nothing to write home about, the woman should insist on paying her half, unless the man has made it clear that he's been looking forward to treating her. In short, most often paying is a question of economic judg-ment where the rules can't be laid down in advance.

There are only a few rules here that are absolute: The woman pays all her incidental expenses—taxis, babysit-ters, panty hose. But if you decide to split the check, split it. Run as fast as you can from anyone who says, "Your

Roquefort dressing was fifty cents extra"; and never assume that your date believes in check-splitting just because you do—it can be disastrous if one of you has enough for half the check while the other has about thirty-five cents.

Financial arrangements become important to a romance, and you'll eventually be able to tell a lot about a man or a woman from his or her reaction to money, but money is too touchy a subject to let it cloud a first date. Here, both parties should make every effort to avoid making the check an issue (you'll see that later both of you will have to go to great lengths to *make* the check an issue). Finally, the guest thanks the host for dinner ("Thank you" is how we do that; and "you're welcome" is, somehow, more graceful a response than "no problem"), and each thanks the other again at the end of the evening.

"Well, ha-ha, if you *don't* sleep together at the end of the evening, doesn't that just end the whole thing right there?" a man asked me the other night at a party. Where, I ask you, did the idea come from that a date automatically ends in bed, the way the sun ends each day by sinking into the western horizon? I left this man chuckling over a drink at his cleverness and went off to ask a woman friend the same question. Her response was perhaps more generous, if a little confusing: "It doesn't matter when you sleep together; I don't really keep track. But Toby and I didn't sleep together until the fifth date."

For a recent book called *Singles*, the authors, Jacqueline Simenauer and David Carroll, surveyed single people to discover their living and courting "patterns," and discovered that an astonishing two-thirds of the men—slightly fewer women—slept together between the first and third dates. (Had they wanted to, they could have been astonished to find that an astonishing one-third, give or take, didn't sleep together until *after* the third date.) These figures seem to me meaningless. There's a world of difference between the strength of your feelings on the first date and the third, for one thing, and besides, a "first date" between people who have known each other for years and one involving virtual strangers aren't in the same category to begin with. By any accounting, courtship these days moves along at a fast clip, but that doesn't mean that anyone should have to adjust his or her sexuality to fit a statistical chart. It also doesn't mean that one is *supposed* to jump into bed by the third date (or be accused of reverse perversion?). It doesn't, in fact, mean much of anything, especially at the end of an evening, when your friend begins to murmur something about slipping into something more comfortable and you feel perfectly comfortable just the way you are.

For the rules that hold a culture together to work at all, they have to fit the facts of that culture. Stoplights in Tibet where there are no cars would make about as much sense as yak lanes would here. The fact is that people sleep together at different times in their courtship sequence, for different reasons and with different hopes. What was once a moral issue (nice girls don't) now means something different with each new set of circumstances.

A "chaperon" was originally a tall pointed hat with a veil (the French word for hat is *chapeau*), and in the Middle Ages both unmarried men and women hid under these veiled hats to ensure chastity. But the hats apparently didn't quite do the trick, because chaperones came to mean, of course, older people, women usually, who protected young girls from young men. Particularly in England where the institution took the strongest hold, they became as much a part of courtship then as IUDs are today, and part of the game of courtship was to devise ways to elude one's chaperone, or one's friend's chaperone. By the end of the Victorian era, when young people had just about had it with chaperones, roller-skating (a sport at which chaperones weren't terribly agile) came into vogue; the institution came to an inevitable end shortly thereafter. But chaperones did provide a wonderful way out for young people when they got to the what-do-I-do-now? point. They would know then that it was time to wake up the chaperone and go home.

Chaperones don't have to be hats or people, of course. Parents imposing curfews are also chaperoning their offspring, or trying to; the sanction on a woman's virginity and the fear of pregnancy were also in their days effective monitors. In my parents' youth, or so the legend goes, the young man who lured a girl into "doing it" understood the implicit promise that if something went wrong he would take the responsibility—if the young woman managed to get pregnant, she'd usually manage to get married as well. In the free-love Sixties and Seventies, however, men and women were hard put to find chaperone-substitutes when they weren't ready to go to bed, and had to make do with such faint protests as, "I'm not ready yet to get involved." Now the closest thing we have to a chaperone is the very real fear of herpes and other venereal nightmares, the very thought of which reminds us that our actions do indeed have consequences.

Still, it's not exactly romantic to say to someone you hope you'll grow to like, "I can't tonight because you might have herpes," the most likely answer to which is, "But I don't." All you're left with is, "Still, I'd feel better if we waited," to which your friend replies, "Well, even if I do have herpes, which I don't, then I'd still have it next time," which leaves the exchange on a dour—instead of an anticipatory—note. Much easier and more romantic to be able to say, "My darling, I must depart forthwith, though it breaks my heart, for my chaperone beckons." I suspect that sooner or later everyone wants to end an evening without ending a relationship—and wishes for a real-live chaperone to come along and take care of the whole thing.

But to understand this isn't always enough when you're seized with end-of-the-evening panic this early in a relationship, when questions and conflicts are shooting around like laser beams in your mind: How do I know this is a relationship? How can I say no without hurting his or her feelings? How can I be sure this person has in mind what I *think* he or she has in mind? What do *I* really want for that matter? What will I think in the morning? What do I do now?

There's also the old residual guilt you might feel if you say yes; *that* guilt's been centuries in the making. And there's the newer contemporary guilt you might feel if you say no: What's wrong with me? What's stopping me from doing this—am I incapable of loving or trusting? Moreover, there is little doubt that it's easier for a man to jump into bed without thinking ahead than it is for a woman. (Who cares whether this is biological or cultural? Some facts are just facts.) Most men I've talked to, however, can easily distinguish between sex and courtship sex, and are at least sympathetic with a dilemma that may finally be more a woman's dilemma.

Whether to sleep with somebody before you are absolutely 100 percent without question certain you want to is a matter of etiquette as much as it is a moral choice. When you're courting the problem is not how to say no to someone with whom you don't want to sleep—there, the manners are clear: "Let's just be friends." The dilemma arises when you want to say no to someone with whom you *do* want to sleep. Or as an Italian philosopher writing about love summed it up, "Modesty is hiding what you care to concede."

In the fifties, Jack Kerouac wrote, "Boys and girls in America have such a sad time together; sophistication demands that they submit to sex immediately without proper preliminary talk. Not courting talk—real straight talk about souls, for life is holy and every moment is precious." Sometimes I think I've done enough talking about souls to last me a lifetime, but I do agree with Kerouac that the *idea* of what it means to be sophisticated can send us bouncing into bed long before we're ready, or at least a date or two early.

There's a symmetry lacking in a date if the man doesn't see the woman to her door, so most men will see their dates home. The same sense of symmetry might make the woman want to invite the man in for a drink or a last cup of coffee. And here is where the trouble usually starts. You're both thinking, "Aha, I know what this is about," and you're as certain of the roles you're expected to play as if you were Olivier getting ready for another Hamlet.

The misconception here is that the man is expected to make a perfunctory pass, and to be insistent enough about it so that the woman will either give in or wrestle him out of the house. Not true. A sincere kiss, if neither of you is ready for more, might be romantic enough so that you'll exchange hearts forever. (At least it could keep you interested until the next date.) Another misconception is that in order to say "no for now" it's better to come up with excuses ("I have to be at work early"; "I'm tired"; "I'm expecting a call from Iran at five in the morning") than it is to be forthright: "I do want to sleep with you, but I'm not ready yet."

If I've come to believe one thing about courtship it's that people, men and women alike, care more about lasting affection than they do about ephemeral sex. There are, of course, occasions in our disordered lives that confuse the issue, occasions when we are likely to take on a beside-the-point lover. Loneliness, a little too much to drink, a friendship that turns momentarily or from time to time into a love affair, the despair of having been rejected by a spouse or lover can lead many of us to lick our wounds in a friend's (or a friendly stranger's) bed now and again. I don't think, though, that lonely sex or friendly sex are the same as what the media like to call casual sex. Most of us don't take sex casually. Anatole France wrote that "Christianity has done much for sex by making it a sin." That, with all its complications, was true for centuries; but for most of us sex isn't a sin anymore. Instead it's the most fundamental and complex gift we have to offer. And when it comes to not casual but courtship sex, saying no can be a gift, too. But the most meaningful gift comes when you both know it's time to say yes.

Chapter Six

The Sleep-Over Date

THEODORE ROOSEVELT first met Alice Lee, who was to become the love of his life, on a Friday in mid-October, 1878, when they were introduced by friends. They met again that Saturday, when they and their friends walked together in the woods near her house in Massachusetts. Later that afternoon, with another group, they drove to visit friends for dinner and tea. On Sunday, alone for the first time, they wandered off after church to pick chestnuts. Three weeks later they saw each other again, and the Lee family invited Roosevelt to Thanksgiving dinner. That night he wrote in his diary, "They call me by my first name now." Had Roosevelt and Lee been courting today instead of a century ago, it's fair to guess that not only would they long since have been on a first name basis—they'd very likely also have been lovers.

Whether it's the first date, the second or the tenth, in a new romance the promise of sex hovers like a mosquito:

You're distracted by it, fascinated, annoyed. You can't wait for it to land, and you can't really concentrate on too much else until the buzzing is out of the way. You try to avoid it, but there it is, and there you are, following it around with your mind.

Little girls, and little boys, too, I imagine, daydream through a Vaseline-covered lens about what the first time will be like. My first-time fantasy is now vague to me, but I do recall a softly lit room with piles of peach-colored cushions, lots of candles. I was beautiful, with long blond hair and blue eyes, my figure out of *Vogue*. So far as I can remember there wasn't anything resembling a man in the room (that part's a puzzle), but he was nearby and he adored me. In any event, the first time could happen only once—in my fantasy, that is.

For most of us, though, the reality is different. The first time does happen more than once, and each time you find yourself on the verge of intimacy it seems like a precarious place to be. Nor is it always possible to be sure that the occasion will turn out to be anything like fantasy-perfect. What happens most often is that we sleep together hoping to find intimacy, not to cement an intimacy that already exists.

"Do you think you'll *sleep* with him tonight?" I once asked a close friend over the phone as she was getting ready to go out with a man she had seen a few times before, someone she really liked. I can't remember her words exactly, but what she said was inspired, pointing to all the excitement, conflict and uncertainty that exist on such occasions. Condensed, it went something like:

I mean, I'd really like to, I want to, I don't know. I don't even know if he would. Plus I'm getting my period, I'm fat today, my apartment's a mess. And we're meeting at the movie—what are we supposed to do, take two cars? If I go to his place, then I have to come home in the morning to wash my hair. I've got to be at the office at eight-thirty. Well, nine. But I really like him, should I bring my diaphragm? But that would look like I brought my dia-phragm....I hope so.

Often, as in my friend's case, the logistics are staggering enough to postpone a love affair for weeks. There can be other worries and doubts, too, that collide with every-thing that makes you want to say yes. "I feel like a virgin every time," a divorced woman, Angela, told me. She went on to say that many of the men she had met since her marriage fell apart had disappointed her: "They're basically decent, attractive people, but you sleep with them and they practically run away after that. Sometimes they don't even call later." Her solution—now she waits longer to start a love affair, and when she does, "Some-times I think they know how tense I feel about it."

Arthur, a single man in his early thirties, finds the first time simply an obstacle to overcome. It's after the first time, he feels, that a love affair really begins. "You can't relax until later, until you really begin to know the person. I just like to get the first time out of the way. What you want is to feel closer after that." And Nancy, a graduate student in New York, has other doubts. "The last time I slept with someone, I got this infection. My doctor said it could have been passed on through the man, and that I should ask the men to wear prophylactics. But how do you ask them to do that?"

A few people, afraid they might not be "good in bed," worried that they wouldn't be as good as a new friend's former lovers. "These single women have been to bed with a lot of people," complained a divorced man in his early forties. "Who knows what kind of sex makes them happy?" Or as the poet Philip Larkin described the anxiety:

> Sexual intercourse began
> In nineteen sixty-three
> (Which was rather late for me)—
> Between the end of the *Chatterley* ban
> And the Beatles' first LP.

Because we all bring a complicated history into the bedroom with us, we can't expect every romance to start with a clean slate. Your feelings will depend on what has happened to you before and on what you would like to see happen now. Not only is sex on your mind. You're also wondering where this is going to lead; what your friend expects to happen; whether your own hopes will be taken seriously. These concerns, combined with the inevitable worries about pregnancy, disease, impotence, performance and cracker crumbs in the bed are the classic elements of both high drama and low comedy.

Naturally you're nervous. "The purpose of sexual intercourse," as the writer Edmund Wilson described it, "and hence of what we call love, is to secure the survival of the human race and, if possible, to improve its breed." The purpose of sexual intercourse is not simply to cool out at the end of a long date. Wilson may have put it a little bluntly for some tastes, but I think that each of us, every time we engage in even the most carefree sex, is aware that our actions are on some level profound.

Where did we ever get the idea that a love affair should begin with as little fuss as possible? that it should appear totally spontaneous, almost as if it were happening to any two people and not particularly to us? All species and cultures surround the act of mating with the most solemn rites, and even for human beings in the 1980s, when sex the first time is so to speak "on approval" with no threats or chains or promises of lifetime commitment, sexual etiquette celebrates the importance of sex and of the man and woman who are making love together.

It's a pity that no one ever thought to include a check-list in every new package of birth-control equipment: "Now that you have your Pills, have you thought of the following? Fresh coffee, towels, sheets, croissants, flowers? Is your date planned with a free morning tomorrow? Did you buy candles, firewood? If you bought firewood, do you have a fireplace?" There are endless ways to heighten the first time, to make it the event you (at least deep down inside) would like it to be.

You don't have to drape a banner—WELCOME, NOR-MAN—across your front door, invest in satin sheets or filmy white negligees to prove to your friend that sleeping with him or her matters to you. Sexual etiquette is private, and subtle. But whether the lovemaking takes place at a time neither of you expected it would or whether, as is more often the case, you both have a pretty good idea that this will be the night, sexual courtesy expresses thoughtfulness and respect as much or more than the most studied foreplay possibly could, particularly if your foreplay is somebody else's idea of twoplay or threeplay.

Those who fail to take the responsibility for a decision as important as the decision to make love—those who say, "Gee, I don't know, it just happened"—often miss the point. Sex, even if it doesn't turn out to be forever sex, is supposed to *matter*. It's also supposed to be, among other things, fun. It's pointless to have gone through all the turmoil of the sexual revolution, of fighting all that

Puritan guilt, if now that we've won we can't appreciate each person separately for the joy he or she might be willing to share.

In the early Sixties, Helen Gurley Brown, now the editor of *Cosmopolitan*, caused a huge commotion with her first book, *Sex and the Single Girl*. I didn't read it at the time, although doubtless I would have found it shocking if I had, but reading it now is mind-blowing—for another reason: There is virtually no mention of sex in *Sex and the Single Girl*. The book deals with diets, apartments, clothes, budgets and careers (if there aren't a lot of men where you work, get a new job). It talks about how not to sleep with a man, and how to be suggestive about it. But it stops short of what happens when the lights go out, in other words, when the really important "procedural" questions arise.

"I can almost always tell when it's going to happen," says Lauren Waters, a twenty-seven-year-old production assistant, who lives in a small studio apartment in New York. "For one thing, I get hysterical." She laughed as she described her preparatory "rituals." "It takes at least six hours to get ready. You have to shave your legs, do your hair, all that, then you try on everything you own to decide what to wear. I always clean my apartment in case he comes here—and switch to a bigger pocketbook (for 'supplies') in case I go there." Most of all, most people I talked to agreed, you have to pretend you haven't "planned" at all, in the same way a host who prepares a lavish dinner for forty claims it was effortless, "nothing at all." Or as Jay, another man I talked to, says, "I guess I do plan. I mean, I make the bed and try to clean up a little."

Evenings like the ones Lauren and Jay describe often "feel" different from other evenings. Knowing that something is going to happen, even if you're not sure exactly when or exactly how it will come about, gives a soft, almost sentimental cast to the hours preceding. There is little to match the intensity of feeling between two people who know they're going to sleep together: "Like Christmas Eve," Jay says. Until, that is, it's time to go home and thus begin the "my place or yours" debate; but where, in an age of peripatetic love, is "home"?

Some people have a homing instinct as strong as E.T.'s. They feel safer at home; they like to be surrounded by their own things: At ten o'clock they have to know where their toothbrushes will be. As my friend Marcy says, "It's a question of territorial imperative. And I think the woman should be able to have the final say. She, after all, is probably the one with the birth control." Another woman, Pat, also finds the birth-control situation delicate: "Even if you're pretty sure you're going to sleep together, who wants to carry around a diaphragm? I know someone who dropped hers once, at a bus stop. She was mortified. I'd rather be home." Matthew, a friend of mine, sees it another way: "It's inconvenient for whoever goes to the other place. You shouldn't have to go somewhere just because the diaphragm's there. That's just an excuse." Others feel shy about arriving home early in the morning, walking past the neighbors or nodding to the doorman. "It's sad to have to think about it, but there's a security guard where I live, and I hate going past him and waving at seven in the morning. It's just not very romantic," a Florida schoolteacher wrote me. "Also, school starts earlier than most other jobs, so why should I always have to get up first?"

Others prefer being the guest to being the host. "You can call the shots if you're somewhere else," a world-weary thirty-year-old man told me. "You can leave when you want. Some women come over and act as if they're

going to stay forever. It makes me feel really closed in."
A slightly younger woman felt the same way: "My apartment's so small to begin with. When someone else is there too I feel like I live in a closet. I'd rather go to his place." Still another guy claimed laziness as the reason he made a better guest. "When you're divorced you're reduced to an Oscar Madison kind of person. Most women would have to clean my apartment before they'd want to sleep there." A friend of mine, who is admittedly battle-scarred, prefers, for emotional reasons, to be the guest. "If I stay at his place then he'll miss me when I'm gone. If it doesn't work out, I don't want to fill my apartment up with memories."

Let's hope that one of you wants to be the host, and the other wants to be the guest. A match made in heaven. The way the world works, however, is that generally one of you says, "Let's go over to my house," and the other either agrees—or says instead, "Oh, why don't we go to *my* house?" A dialogue not so offhand as it sounds. But don't let the issue reach an impasse. And don't worry that if you give in now you'll be setting an irreversible precedent; irreversible precedents don't get set until the next chapter. It's polite to insist on your way this time *only* if you have a real reason to. If you do, say simply, "I'd much prefer it if we...." You're not obliged to give the details. Be willing to give in if your "reason" is only your own comfort; in fairness, you'll have your turn to be comfortable next time.

Once you get to the "there" you're going to, whichever one it is, don't be afraid to see that your guest is put at ease and feels as much at home as possible. It's easy to be lonely, to feel out of place at a new lover's house. If your sixth sense has given you notice, it's lovely (no, it's not too obviously seductive) if you've prepared for the evening as you would for any other houseguest—clean sheets, fresh towels, even flowers. In a pinch, just hide the clutter, especially clean clutter hanging in various odd places to dry, as best you can.

More important, draw your guest into your home; you are, after all, about to draw him or her into your bed. Have his or her customary drink available; play a record your friend really likes, or a favorite of your own: "I'd really like you to hear this." Pull out a book, a tennis racket, a cooking gadget, any show-and-tell item to talk about to remind you both that you have a reason to be there together. It's not enough to walk in the door and say, "Just make yourself at home." Nothing freezes people in place faster than that. Whatever you do, don't dump your friend on the sofa while you go off to do something else.

"Women get nervous," says a friend of mine, "and you've got to find diversions and distractions. Sometimes I take off my shoes—just doing that seems casual. Or have her help you look for something. Get the drinks together." Another woman suggests something I would not have thought of myself (and would recommend only with reservations): "Do something fun first. The first time my boyfriend came over we played hopscotch on the kitchen floor. It was dumb, but it calmed us both down."

One of the standard rules for keeping marriages together is never argue in bed; married people can argue as much as they like, experts agree, but they should do it practically anyplace but in bed. At this point in a courtship it's too early to argue, certainly too early to be tempted to argue in bed, but it's wise to settle the "red tape" of lovemaking before you find yourself in the bedroom. If you have to go home before morning, for example, bring it up now, while you're still "playing" ("This is really fun; I wish I didn't have to go home later to take out the dog."). Bring up anything else pertinent your friend should know ahead of time. And the most important subject to get out of the way, unpleasant as it is to contemplate, is that of sexually transmitted diseases. As a friend of mine half-joked during the first media blitz about herpes, "I'm terrified—I wish I could buy a VD detector."

Old as the risk of VD is, it's particularly stupid today to ignore the possibilities of contracting any one of the several such diseases around. The fact that herpes was recently a *Time* magazine cover story should be enough to convince anyone that even the nicest people are not immune. As I interviewed people for this book, it was heartbreaking to run into men and women—any of whom could have been you or me—who had "gotten something" from a friend; the confusion, guilt and unhappiness that resulted *must* be prevented, and this requires an effort on the part of everyone who is sexually active. Most heartbreaking of all is that people who do catch things very often do so from friends who don't know they have a problem. As for people who would knowingly expose another person to such a disease, they are in a class by themselves, but I ran across hardly anyone who suspected that he or she had been deceived about this by a lover. Most people I talked to felt that their friends had been unwitting victims, just as they had become in turn. Thus a clean bill of health from a lover-to-be might not be enough. Or your friend might be a passive carrier.

This is more than a question of etiquette, and I am beginning to hear about more and more men and women who choose to use prophylactics at first, not simply for birth control but to prevent disease. In a new relationship, any inconvenience here is more than balanced by the peace of mind such a precaution can bring to you both.

The question is how to bring it up without sounding impossibly clinical or even mildly accusatory about it.

If you'd feel safer using a condom, apologize if you have to for suggesting it; blame it on your own worries, a story you heard from a friend or this book. Blame it on the unreliability of whatever other birth control is around. Don't pursue the subject any more than necessary—"I like you a lot, and I'd feel terrible if anything happened to wreck this. Could we...." It sounds like such a touchy thing to do—but it won't be, once more of us grow accustomed to the idea. (No one trusted automobiles in the beginning, either.) Your only other option is trust, an option not to be discounted, but as we've seen, one that isn't always dependable. There is simply no graceful way to say, "Hey, you don't have any diseases or anything, do you?" There's a joke that goes: What's the difference between herpes and love? The answer is that unlike love, herpes lasts forever. It's a pretty sad joke—but it can turn out to be even sadder when otherwise self-respecting people aren't cautious about their health.

A final note about this. I'm not a doctor and so can't tell you how to prevent, recognize or treat these diseases, but I think it's important to learn as much as we can about them—and part of what we need to learn is compassion. As I write this, herpes, for which there is no cure, is the biggest cause for alarm, but herpes victims are not creatures from outer space and should not be treated as if they were. One of the most touching stories I heard was from a young woman who has been going out with the same man for close to a year now. "The first time we went to bed together, he told me he had herpes, but that it was okay, it wasn't in an active phase. I remember thinking how nice he was to tell me the truth. He also said that he'd never do anything to hurt me, and that you usually *know* when it's going to be most contagious. And that he'd never make love then. I felt really close to him. It hasn't been a problem."

Phew. Now you are ready to begin.

Your first responsibility when it comes to actual sex is to have your osculogical and philametological skills in order, and to recognize your impulses as you move from tumescence to contrection and then to detumescence. All of which is to say not to worry too much about the technicalities of sex.

Because it's more enjoyable and universal than anything else you can think of, sex was one of the first subjects mankind considered seriously; the study of sex began, for example, long before the invention of synfuel. The science of kissing was documented both by the Greeks (who called it osculogy; see above) and the Romans (who gave it a longer name, philametology). Later, the Germans categorized kissing even further, and discovered thirty kinds of it, listed under separate entries in their dictionaries. Orientals fell behind on this one—from the beginning they thought kissing was disgusting, something that only cannibals did.

Sometime between the discovery of kissing thousands of years ago and the more recent discovery of performance anxiety, Havelock Ellis, the famous sex expert who died in 1938, believed that sex had three phases: tumescence (the genital urge); contrection (he must have liked the sound of this one, picked up from another researcher, Albert Moll; it means emotional arousal, which of course is not absolutely necessary for every kind of sex); and detumescence, which is, of all things, the wonderful feeling that comes after sex. The sexual labeling that took place earlier in this century was an important step toward giving big scary names to ordinary, familiar and very human impulses. Going along with Ellis for the moment, though, tumescence is more or less a reflex; whether you're a man or a woman your body knows when it's aroused. The emotional urge, assuming for the sake of discussion that the two can be so easily distinguished and isolated, is more delicate.

If you've come this far toward starting a love affair, both your body and your mind should agree that this is really what you want to do. To have sex like a grownup is to be free about it, and to be as decisive and certain as you can be. It's not unnatural to feel doubtful at the last minute, but these are *your* doubts, and it's not fair to go overboard about passing them on to your friend, who very likely is grappling with doubts of his or her own.

People have long believed that at the beginning women put more importance on the emotional aspects of sex, while men pay greater attention to their physical urges, and think about the emotional stuff later. I'm sure that's true—and I think that both men and women would be happier lovers if from the beginning we all remembered that. Let's take Max, who says, "Melinda, you have the most beautiful body." Believing that he and Melinda are on the same sexual wavelength, he'll expect her to understand that this is the most important compliment he can give her at this moment. Poor Max. Melinda, who's preoccupied more with emotions just now and wonders how he feels about her as a "person," may well react by thinking, "I knew it. He just wants me for my body," suspecting that because he's just mentioned her body this is all he really cares about. She may say in reply, reflecting her own uncertainties, "I don't usually sleep with people this early," or, "Are you sure we should be doing this?" It's the commonest thing in the world that at the beginning he's looking for physical reassurance while what she wants more is emotional support.

What Max might say instead, to address Melinda's need for assurance that he's thinking of more than her body, is up to Max. Melinda, too, should have a script of her own to assure Max that she's eager to have sex with him. Whatever the dialogue, there are deep chasms differentiating the way women think from the way men think and this is central to sexual etiquette. By this I don't mean that you should parrot what you think your friend wants to hear. But I do mean that a gentle lover pays attention, in a sort of equal-time way, to both emotional and physical needs, and comforts his or her lover when he or she seems to feel insecure.

Sexual etiquette is far more than a working knowledge of genital mechanics: It's presenting yourself generously to a lover, insofar as you're able. Letting your lover see that you're sincere and hopeful is an awesome and trusting thing to be able to do, far more telling than jumping into bed and "doing" it. As a friend of mine said about herself, "I never took myself seriously until I traded in the bed I had as a kid for a double bed." Her observation says more than it appears to, for it was then that she became, as she put it, a "real woman," and that her relations with men started for the first time to become adult relations.

"Sometimes you're nervous and the first time isn't so great," says a thirty-one-year-old management consultant from San Francisco. "Other times it can blow your ears off." "The anticipation makes it exquisite," a medical student from Chicago wrote in his questionnaire, "but it gets better once you're used to each other." A curator from Washington says she "concentrates more on the man the first time. I keep wondering whether he's enjoying it." Another woman, a friend of mine who lives in Michigan, says she "holds back at first. I'm sort of afraid to have an orgasm until I see if there's going to be a second time." The pleasures—and the difficulties—of the first time are unique. Because newness intensifies lovemaking, you'll both sense a pressure to make the whole thing perfect. But nothing is perfect, and real life sometimes joins us, uninvited, in the bedroom.

The *couvade*, the sympathetic childbirth pains men sometimes feel, is taken seriously enough to be given an anthropological name—why, then, isn't there a name to suggest that women can suffer sympathetically too when a man is impotent? Granted, impotence is first and foremost a man's dilemma, but when a woman confronts it, it becomes her problem, too. Think of it this way: Women have faced impotence exactly as many times as heterosexual men have. It's an obstacle to lovemaking that the sexes share.

The first thing sensitive lovers should realize about impotence is that it's not a secret. What scientists call secondary impotence—the occasional failure of erection that comes from nervousness, fatigue, perhaps one drink too many—has been written about widely. A woman would have had to grow up on Saturn not to have heard about it, and she might even have experienced impotence as many times as the man she's with. Believe me, unless she spent her life not only on Saturn but in a convent on Saturn, she knows what's going on.

Most of the men and women I've talked to agree that it's up to the man to acknowledge when he is, for the moment, impotent; there is simply no tactful way for the woman to mention it first. The longer he waits, the more frustrating and awkward the situation will become—for both. Until you can both discuss the problem, you have to go on pretending that it doesn't exist (something like the emperor's new clothes). As a result, you'll feel farther and farther apart—unless the man lets the woman know, as simply as he can. as soon as he knows himself.

The worst way a man can tell a woman is by saying, "This has never happened to me before," even if it hasn't, because, as Margaret, a woman I recently met, says, "Then you'll just wonder, 'Oh, no, what have I done wrong now?'" Nobody should be made to feel guilty. The truth, something like, "I've been looking forward to this, but now that we're here I guess I'm just nervous," is fine. Many men agree that simplicity on the woman's part— "I'm nervous, too, but mostly I'm just glad you're here"— is the best solution as well. I talked to a man named Carl, who advises, "Don't keep saying over and over that it's okay. That sounds like protesting too much." Too much compassion, too earnestly expressed, makes a bigger deal of impotence than it is. And don't go too far the other way, either, says Scott, who told me about a woman who greeted his impotence with silence. "It was awful, she just didn't say anything. Maybe she didn't know what to say. But I wish she'd said *something*. That silence made me feel really strange."

Anxiety aside, there can be something touching about impotence. As Stendhal wrote in *Love*, "Perhaps men who cannot love passionately are those who feel the effect of beauty most keenly; at any rate this is the strongest impression women can make on men." And many women *do* find that there's something especially poignant about first-time impotence. One woman with whom I talked found it touching in a man who later became her "roommate." They spent the first night affectionately, and by morning, when the problem miraculously had cured itself, both felt as if their worries had dissipated during the night. Another man told a woman I know, "The only other time this happened to me was the first time I slept with my ex-wife." She was enchanted. And a friend of mine recently married a woman whom he had dated for nearly three years. He was impotent for the first time on their wedding night. They both found it hilarious and romantic.

Genital malfunctions are not so noticeable in a woman, but things can go wrong for her, too, and cause considerable smaller-scale anguish. The woman who is menstruating, for example, might feel nervous about how her friend feels about it (most men, by the way, told me they feel fine about it), or about soiling the sheets. A woman who does not become well lubricated before intercourse might feel that she has "failed." Some women feel inadequate if they don't have an orgasm the first time, and may wonder whether to fake one. To a woman, these concerns can be as big a worry as a man's impotence.

"I've had women apologize to me for everything from cellulite to sweating," a friend told me, "but I wish they wouldn't worry so much." Like impotence or the other big worry, premature ejaculation, all these concerns are ordinary hazards and should be handled with compassion and delicacy. If a woman feels uncomfortable about something, she might mention what's making her nervous; then it's up to the man to console her, briefly and gently, just as she'd console him if something went wrong on the other side of the bed.

A friend of mine decided that when his young son turned seven, he was old enough to learn the fundamentals of sex. The man approached the subject warily, but his son had already put two and two together: "Sex? That's sleeping together. The woman has a diagram [sic], and then the man puts his penis into her vagina and they go to sleep." My friend had to concede that his son had grasped at least the fundamentals. But knowing more or less where the sky is doesn't make you an astronomer.

The *Kama Sutra*, the Hindu book of love, was *the* dirty book when I was growing up; a copy in your possession could guarantee you popularity for at least a week. As its allure suggests, the book is a graphic how-to guide for every kind of sex imaginable. Unlike our more crass contemporary version, *The Joy of Sex*, the *Kama Sutra* gives instructions for nurturing intimacy along with its directions for where to put your arms, legs and sundry other bodily parts. Its theory, I guess, is that sex for its own sake is a witless pastime—that it means little without love, and that love takes time. The *Kama Sutra* makes a big deal out of courtship and first-time lovemaking; the first time, it says, should be brief and simple, with more attention given to fore- and afterplay. You'll feel freer to experiment after you're intimate. I've run into people who disagree, but what most people I've talked to remember about each first time is what happens before lovemaking and, more important, how they feel after, just like the *Kama Sutra* says. Passionate and exciting as the first time might be, it's too charged with emotions and questions to fit easily into the memory. Often it passes almost in a blur. But when it's over you're changed. Your nervousness has gone; you see the world with a new clarity. What we never forget are those rare moments after making love for the first time with someone special.

"Oatmeal cookies." One woman wrote in her questionnaire that she wasn't quite certain whether it fell under the category of "sexual etiquette" but that she had been delighted when a friend brought oatmeal cookies to bed after they'd made love the first time. Others remembered nights when, in a borrowed T-shirt or robe, they stayed up for hours talking, or got dressed and went out for a late-night pizza. Some people are tired afterward, and prefer just to curl up together and go to sleep. What's universal, though, is the need to celebrate what's just happened—and to hold on to the feelings of closeness.

This closeness is fragile, though, and some people have found that a lover's thoughtlessness following sex can bring the mood to an abrupt halt.

"I couldn't believe it," said a twenty-three-year-old woman, Delia, describing the first man she met after moving to New York from a small town in the Midwest. "This guy said he was a poet, and right after making love he jumped—literally—out of bed and ran to his typewriter. I know better than to think my thighs are good material for a poem. I felt really stupid, and I didn't think he was so bright, either." Edward, a divorced man in his mid-thirties with two children of his own, had a different tale of woe: "It was right out of *Kramer vs. Kramer.* She told me her child never woke up during the night. *All* children wake up during the night. And there he was, singing a Christmas carol in the next room, and humming. She was in a custody case and kind of hysterical—she asked me to wait in the closet til he went to sleep. She was afraid he'd wander in; I was afraid I'd never get out."

A more general complaint is the telephone; nothing shatters intimacy faster than an inopportune call, particularly from an inopportune person. Immediately following sex is no time to check in with your answering service or talk at length on the phone or even, if such calls can be postponed, with your children or business associates. (They'll inevitably ask what you're doing, and you'll inevitably say either, "Nothing," or, "Oh, I've got this friend over," and neither will make your naked companion feel very welcome.) The best phone during lovemaking is one that's unplugged. This is also not the time to turn on the radio for the news, or the television to find out whether Chris Evert-Lloyd won her match and you won your bet.

It's also not the time to review the performance as if you were a movie critic. If women's noses grew six feet every time they lied to the did-you-come? question the first time, my guess is that, sexual revolution or no sexual revolution, plastic surgeons would rule the world. Men should realize by now that many women (my instinct, backed by the women I talked with, is to say *most* women) do not reach orgasm the first time. Fact.

I know that men have been ingrained with the notion that a woman must reach orgasm, and that it is his re-sponsibility to see that she does. And I know that in asking, a man is expressing his concern. Still, a good many of us would prefer that he ask the second time, say, or the third. A woman, particularly in the beginning, can feel that the sex was good, that she liked it, that she's feeling happy, without having reached orgasm. "If they ask, I lie the first time," explains Elise, who, once a ro-mance gets going, has little trouble reaching orgasm. "Who wants to go into orgasmic eccentricities right away?"

On the up side, there are plenty of good-manner-ly things you *can* do for your guest. "It makes me feel secure to be asked which side of the bed I like," several people told me, and there are other courtesies as well that prove the little things are really what matter. Giving your guest the choice of pillows or extra blankets; checking to see whether he or she prefers the window open or closed; providing hangers; asking what time to set the alarm clock—all these gestures will be appreciated. Several other people mentioned the romance of a specially run bath. . . .

You will find that your new lover's bathroom is a source of wonder and surprise. This, you'll think, is the toothbrush she brushes her teeth with morning and night, and here are her cotton balls. Imagine, his razor and comb. Even so, don't give into the instinctual temptation to open the medicine cabinet—sadly enough, there is no such thing as a medicine cabinet that closes quietly.

One of the unsolved etiquette problems of our day is whether to share your toothbrush with a friend or offer a brand-new one. There are two schools of thought here: One says that a new one is a thoughtful gesture, and the other says it makes it look as if the host has an endless supply of toothbrushes for just such occasions. A couple of toothbrushes with bristles reasonably intact should see you through this one; a towel of one's own, nearly everyone I consulted agreed, is less negotiable. Provide a fresh towel, no matter what—even if it says "Sal's Boarding-house" on it.

Once, when my apartment was being painted, I stayed for a couple of nights in a friend's spare bedroom. I had forgotten shampoo, and he directed me to a cabinet in which I found the most extravagant collection of female equipment imaginable. It was as if I'd wandered into the cosmetics section of an opulent department store, and I dragged him in to see. "Oh, yeah," he said, "they're from here and there. I thought someone might be able to use them." Mistake. Everyone will be grateful for the basics—the use of a razor, shampoo, hairdrier, a robe—but to see history through a motley collection of used lotions, powders and colognes is unsettling, like attending a sé-ance. (Included here are spare boxes of tampons, which a number of women who found them in men's apartments found distressing.) Or, as a friend of mine says, "'Trace elements.' They belong in the wastebasket."

Medieval lovers, if they were rich enough, would ar-range for a trusted servant to sing an aubade, a dawn-song, to wake them up, so that the man could get out before he got caught by the lady's husband or parents. Popular ideas to the contrary, more lovers have probably ridden off into the sunrise than into the sunset. Starting a love affair properly takes all night and into the morning. Happily, for some idiosyncratically human reason, the "sleeping" part of sleeping together is especially important to most of us.

If you can't arrange to stay together all night, don't just sail out the door tossing an "I'll see ya" over your shoulder. If you do, you deserve to be hit by the flying oranges your friend, who planned to squeeze fresh juice for you in the morning, is aiming at your head.

The hours following lovemaking are for many of us a time for reassurance that what we've done makes sense. A recently vacated half a bed isn't much reassurance. To leave unceremoniously, or to be ejected without fanfare into the night, will too easily be construed as a denial of what's happened between you. This is not to suggest false promises of undying love: Disingenuousness can also start the oranges flying, and rightly so. But it's heartless to leave in a way that makes your lover wonder whether you'll ever meet again. No matter when you part, it's up to the man to promise to call again—and to keep his promise. If you can't spend the night together, the thoughtful man will call the woman the minute he gets home, or if she's the one who has had to leave, he'll call her the minute he estimates she'll arrive home. A warm telephone is obviously no excuse for a warm body, but it's better than nothing.

Leaving in the middle of the night is clearly worse than leaving either earlier in the evening or the following morning. But sometimes it's unavoidable. Perhaps you meant to leave earlier and fell asleep. Or you can't sleep, as a man I interviewed told me he discovered one night when he was confronted by his friend's cats. "Dozens of them," he exaggerated. Or maybe you get claustrophobic. "I didn't know what was going on," another man told me. "We had already talked about where we'd have breakfast and I woke up when I heard her getting dressed. I almost said something, but I didn't, so she could leave in peace." The woman called the next day to apologize; nevertheless, the man felt hurt. The consensus is that, yes, it's better to wake your companion to explain that you're leaving, to save confusion, worry or hurt feelings later. And leave a note as well (a warm note...).

But ideally you'll spend the night and have a civilized breakfast together before deciding what happens next. Weekdays are touchy, as most people have to go home and change clothes before facing the day, even if they're wearing one of those "what to wear on Tuesday if you won't be home til Wednesday" numbers. But try to allow time for at least a cup of coffee, to give yourselves the chance to recapture the feelings of the night before. On weekends, to relax the intense atmosphere of a new affair, many people like to go out to breakfast. "I couldn't make breakfast at home anyway," one guy told me. "The only thing that's been in my refrigerator for the past six months is a thing of yogurt, which by now looks like a science project." And breakfast out is at the same time wonderfully public and absolutely private.

Afterwards, many people feel the need to be alone, to relive the night before or simply for renewal, R and R. Others have a less specific need for privacy. It's difficult, however, for people who don't know each other well to distinguish between "I would like to be alone now" and "I don't really want to be with you now." To avoid misunderstanding, announce your departure plans before breakfast, so that your leaving will not seem sudden or contrived. "I have plans to watch the football game this afternoon with my friend Erroll," or, "I can't believe I have to work all day"—whatever. A man I talked to went out with a woman who looked particularly stricken when he announced that he had plans for the afternoon, and he did what seems to me an especially gracious thing, asking her out to dinner for the following night, even though he hadn't planned to see her again quite so soon.

It's this ability to empathize with what the other person is feeling that defines sexual etiquette and proves that you didn't learn your manners in bootcamp. Thus I was appalled (and I am appalled by very little) to hear time and again about men who after sex had promised to call and didn't. Or about those who, not "realizing" that the promise is implicit, neither promised nor called. This is unbelievably hurtful. Few courtship rules are so clearcut as the rule that the man must call afterward, and soon, even if one or both of you has had second thoughts about the future.

An acquaintance once told me about a habit her ex-husband had that irritated her constantly. He would refer to an event in the past as one that had happened "the other day," whether it happened two days or seven years ago. Such a perspective doesn't help to define how "soon" to make the follow-up call. To a politician soon means one thing; to a woman another. "Soon" in this case is a day, more or less. She's not a three-hour horseback ride away, after all. Even if you're suddenly struck with laryngitis you can always say it with flowers, which is not a bad idea anyway and which, now that I think of it, might make a pretty good Constitutional amendment since we didn't get the ERA passed.

We're way beyond the eighteenth-century French quirk that insisted that a girl who showed any signs of sexual passion be submitted to bloodletting as a cure. We're even beyond the days when the design of the back seat of a car was as important as how the front seat was designed. There are few no-no's anymore. About ten years ago a survey showed how many single partners a single adult had over the course of a year. The figures were seven and four for men and women respectively. Even if that figure is off by a lot, the number shows at least that people don't "play" at sex with a new partner every day or every week. The "Hey, wow, sex" days of the early sexual revolution, if they ever really existed, are over. Whether after the first time you'll end up platonic friends, virtual enemies or even married, each first time counts.

At their best, first times bring together feeling and fantasy, conjuring romantic scenes that in a movie would make you reach for a handkerchief. Sitting cross-legged drinking Tab in her New York apartment, Christina, for example, described to me the beginning of a love affair that had really mattered to her. "After the third date we both wanted to make love and couldn't, because Nick's son was staying with him. I remember he said, 'Next time.' We had a dinner date after that, and he showed up with shuttle tickets to Boston and a reservation at a really nice hotel. We had champagne in our room, it was so elegant. Then we made love and took the shuttle back in the morning." My friend Joe tells the story of a Saturday afternoon when he and his friend Julia took a picnic lunch, the first of the spring, to a pretty spot on a nearby lake. "It was so romantic there, you know how it's warm and cool at the same time? We both wanted to make love. I thought we'd go straight home, but she said no, and we went all over town, buying candles and steaks and wine for dinner—planning for the whole evening. By the time we finally got to bed I was truly in love." Another man, James, who looks as though he doesn't have a romantic bone in his body, remembers a woman with whom he "made love practically all night. Then we slept for awhile and made love again. She had to leave really early to go to a class or something, and I got back into bed and sort of looked around." Pausing to search a minute for the right words to explain the transformation in his bedroom, even his life, he said, "It was like she was still there. I was flooded with wonder at the whole thing."

Chapter Seven

The Honeymoon

MEAD IS a wine made from honey, and in Scandinavian countries it used to play an important part in the marriage ritual. After the wedding night a couple would toast each other with this honey-wine every night throughout one full cycle of the moon; the golden spirits were said to assure good luck, fertility, health and so on. Honey-wine for a month. Honey-month. Honeymoon.

Every culture has its counterpart to this period of private ceremony. That is, every culture recognizes that once sexual initiation has begun, a man and woman must adjust to their new situation in private. Our own honeymoon custom, of course, is a wedding trip, but its real purpose, to ease a couple gradually—and privately—into the mysteries of marriage and sex, is largely forgotten. For most of us, the honeymoon trip has become little more than a swell excuse for a vacation to recover from the trauma of the wedding. Sexual intimacy, and the real honeymoon that accompanies it, takes place much earlier in courtship.

This de facto honeymoon begins after you've slept together a couple of times and have decided that yes, there is something to pursue here. The familiar symptoms of falling in love are, like a head cold, all consuming. You're endlessly energetic, not minding chores that only a week ago seemed so tedious. Your house is cleaner. Your appetite for sex exceeds your appetite for Cheez Doodles. Possibly you lose weight, or feel compelled to buy new clothes, a new record album or a new perfume, something to commemorate what seems to be a new life. One woman I talked to buys a new diaphragm each time she starts a new love affair; my friend Jack notices on his credit card vouchers that he tips like a king when he has a new love. You're at the same time exhilarated and scared to death, and you keep repeating to yourself, usually as you're getting ready to go out yet again, all the reasons why this is a ridiculous idea and will never work. In fact, falling in love is not so different from falling out of a tree; neither, at any rate, gives you much time to think.

All of a sudden you might be spending three, four, five nights a week together. The air is charged with energy, sensuality and discovery. You're finding out what you have in common, where your lives fit together. "You saw that movie? That was my favorite movie of all time and no one else has ever heard of it!" "I can't believe you don't like sausage on your pizza. Neither do I." "You went to Camp Spaghettio? That's amazing: my third cousin went to camp only eight hundred miles from there." "Chocolate's my favorite, too."

In the past, one couldn't get very far into courtship without meeting the other person's family and friends and without knowing all about his or her social standing, religion, financial prospects, everything one had to know to decide whether the match was suitable and should be allowed a chance. The very last thing a couple would learn about each other was what it would be like in bed together. One saw one's intended first through the eyes of the world, in the broad context of public life. Until the honeymoon, one had to guess at or imagine the rest. It wasn't until it was too late to back out, until the honeymoon that is, that Homer had the legendary shock of seeing Bessie with her head full of curlers and her face obscured by cold cream, or that Bessie saw for the first time Homer's rings—such as those around the collar and tub.

Now we do it all backward, putting the honeymoon with all its pleasures and horrors right up front. One of the first things you'll learn about your lover is whether he or she squeezes the toothpaste tube from the middle, and where the cap ends up. Typically you'll see how your lover looks and acts first thing in the morning (which probably led to the invention of electric curlers) before you see how he or she behaves with the family over tea. You'll learn all about your lover's "other" life, life away from you, mostly from what he or she tells you about it. It might be some time before you see for yourself whether Igor's father is as mean as Igor says; if Cecelia is really so gregarious at a party; if Digby, Igor's old friend from prep school, is the funny guy he's made out to be; or whether Cecelia's kids are, in truth, the prodigies you've been told about. Your friend will visualize your "other" world, too, from what you say about it.

What this means is that during the honeymoon you're creating a "third world"—your world together—while you get your bearings sexually and emotionally. If you're completely new to each other you have everything to learn. Even if you knew each other previously, in a more casual way, you're still retreating from the rest of the world now that you've "found" this person, as if for the first time. And this retreat makes a lot of sense.

For one thing, you don't want to sound like the boy who cried wolf, alerting your family, friends, colleagues and Christmas-card list that you're in love, until you're convinced the love is real. Even though you and Lucinda are sleeping together, you can't possibly know her very well this soon. Naturally you don't want to drag her down to Florida to meet your parents: They have wedding rings in their eyes the way cartoon characters plotting stage-coach robberies have dollar signs in theirs. It's also too soon for Lucinda to introduce you to the children from her first marriage. The last thing she wants is for them to grow attached to you before she does. And even when your closest friends (whom you probably haven't seen much since your honeymoon began) want to spend an evening with you and meet Lucinda, you find yourself saying, "Right, we'll get together soon," without making immediate plans to do so.

Part of the reason for this distance—you and Lucinda so far from the rest of the world—is that as adults most of us have been hurt before, and most of us have hurt someone else. We're wary about love. Although we don't consciously think of it this way, the honeymoon is a time for self-protection. We make a private commitment before going public. Knowing that the more enmeshed you and your friend become in each other's lives the more difficult and painful it will be should you part makes you even more guarded. No point, your subconscious tells you, in getting all worked up about this before it's necessary.

More than that, being on a honeymoon takes up enormous amounts of time and energy. The two of you are together in the private world you've created, in perfect pitch. For a time, sometimes for a long time, this intensity is self-sustaining. The rest of the world (i.e., reality) pales by comparison to the excitement of what you're discovering about each other. You're covering a lot of emotional ground quickly—that "too much, too soon" feeling—and you're magnetized by that invisible "thing" that seems to be pulling you together. You have little time, you feel, for much else. Besides, you're having fun.

Just as you're learning new things all the time about your companion, so too are you seeing yourself in a new way. Your lover points out qualities about you that few people notice: She sees, perhaps, that you're not the tough guy most people think; unlike other men you've known, he admires you for being strong and not a bubblehead. You try this new "self" of yours on for size. We're different people every time we fall in love.

A man I know, Thomas, went out with the same woman, Joanne, for about three years. To the rest of us they always seemed to be having a terrific time, zooming around town in a rickety old convertible and living together in a ramshackle but comfortable old house they rented. They loved discovering lively, inexpensive places to go for dinner or to listen to music, and searching out theaters that showed classic old movies. They were lucky, too, at finding the kind of secondhand shops that never seem to be open when *I* find them. They suddenly broke up, or at least it appeared sudden, and a couple of years later Thomas ended up marrying another woman. But by then he was a different Thomas. He drove a serious car for the first time. He began wearing three-piece suits, and he and his wife moved into a starkly modern condominium. (Frankly, Thomas by now had become pretty boring.) The change was both startling and baffling. The real Thomas must have been a little of each of these Thomases. He changed personalities when he changed partners.

Various expressions we have point this out: "Jeremy is a new man since he met Morticia"; "That Harry really brings out the best in Timidia" or, "I've never seen Genevieve so calm before." Carly Simon sings a song that goes something like, "whoever you want me to be I'll be," but that's only part of it. It's natural to want to please your lover, to do everything you can to make him or her happy. More mystifying, though, is the way that, when people start pairing off in twos, the chemistry of one mixes curiously with that of the other (as you can see, I didn't major in chemistry) and presto, each one feels like a different person.

Perhaps in your last relationship you were the one to shower first in the morning while Drudgina was out in the kitchen making your waffles. Now, with Natalie, you find yourself whistling about the kitchen in your robe, gathering the newspaper from the porch and starting the coffee perking as you hear her shower going full blast. When it comes your turn, you don't seem to mind that you have to slide across the bathroom floor to reach the shower, or that when you've arrived you find that all the hot water is in beads on the bathroom mirror. Or possibly you never before owned so much as a fork and a month ago would not have thought to have dinner at home. But now that you've met Waldo you're content to spend most nights wandering rapturously around the kitchen, throwing a "few things together" for supper so that the two of you can spend a quiet evening alone. Maybe you've stopped swearing or taken up dancing. You might be more reflective than usual, or more cheerful. Honeymoon.

You're probably muttering in confusion to yourself

that "this isn't like me." But it's through intense experimentation with different people that you learn about love and about what you can expect from others. It's also from love that you'll figure out a good deal about who *you* are. Suppose you meet Seaworthy, the first man to tell you you're beautiful. You believe him, and for the first time you're seeing yourself as beautiful, and acting with the confidence of a beautiful woman. By the time you and Seaworthy break up, shortly after his annual eye checkup, you're certain that you're beautiful, so that when you meet Backhand beauty is no longer one of your hangups. Backhand praises your cooking, your canned ravioli with your special touch—a pinch of dried oregano—and all of a sudden you're not only beautiful, you're also a great cook. (If you're smart you'll keep away from Rattail, who could point out that your hair is hopeless and that bottled Italian dressing is something he wouldn't serve to his dog.) There's much more involved in defining the self, of course, but love—the love of family, friends, lovers—always works like a mirror: It puts you face to face with yourself, under every kind of light.

All of this is well and good. You're learning about yourself and your lover; you're having the most romantic time of your life; you're feeling great. Your life is on track, after all. But you won't be able to live forever in a honeymoon bubble. Amid all the fun you're having, you and your lover are thinking about post-honeymoon matters, and the idyllic present is full of clues about what's in store for your future.

Etiquette from out of the past doesn't give us much advice about how new lovers should behave—horrors—so long before marriage. Instead, the "rules" at work here are those that you and your lover will establish for your relationship as you go along, both now in the midst of your honeymoon and later. You are, in effect, laying the foundation for a romance whose future at this point is fuzzy. It's going to be a while before you can tell for certain whether you're building your shelter on a plot of quicksand or on solid ground, or even what kind of shelter it is you're building. In his novel *The Book of Laughter and Forgetting*, the Czech writer Milan Kundera describes what's happening:

> To put it another way, every love relationship is based on unwritten conventions rashly agreed upon by the lovers during the first weeks of their love. On the one hand, they are living a sort of dream; on the other, without realizing it, they are drawing up the fine points of their contracts like the most hard-nosed of lawyers. O lovers! Be wary during those first perilous days! If you serve the other party breakfast in bed, you will be obliged to continue the same in perpetuity or face charges of animosity and treason.

Among the responsibilities to be doled out for your "contract" are the practical day-to-day details of running a romance. No, a love affair will not run forever on sex and good times. Someone has to cook when you're together, and someone has to clean up. Beds have to be made, tickets picked up, reservations taken care of, movie schedules researched, transportation arranged. Someone has to think up things to do, and someone else has to agree to do them. Setting up these everyday "rules" is partly something that just happens, as both of you respond to cues, giving a little, taking a little. But you had better be aware that you *are* setting precedents, that when the honeymoon is over you may decide you don't really *want* to cut up the onions every time.

A friend of mine early on got into the habit of making the bed at her boyfriend's house. "I just started making it one day, and kept on doing it. I wasn't dying to or anything; I just didn't mind." A year later something snapped. "I just didn't want to make the damn bed. It's his bed anyway; why should I have to do it all the time? What annoys me most is the way he just *assumes* the bed will get made."

Another woman, one who works with me, once, in the first throes of love, came dashing into my office. "Quick," she said, "I need an easy recipe for fish." This woman happens to be really proud that Chicken Tarragon is the only dish she knows how to make and, man or no man, that's the way she has always wanted to leave it. She hates to cook. "How about Chicken Tarragon?" I suggested. "I made that on Tuesday," she said. To my recollection, she made Fish Tarragon that night, Pork Chops Tarragon the following week, Eggs Tarragon for lunch on Sunday. The affair ended soon after tarragon season: The tacit "cooking" contract she had got herself into was obviously one of the things that had started the relationship irreparably on the wrong foot.

Nelson, a man I interviewed recently, caught on right away to the idea of precedents. "I don't mind doing the dishes or cleaning up, and I'm not a bad cook," he said, as he described the beginning of his love affair with a woman called Edie. "One night we were making dinner. I was doing most of it—she, I remember, was arranging shrimps on plates. I said, 'The one thing I really hate to do is empty the garbage,' which I really do hate to do. I was hoping she'd offer to do it, but she said, 'Me, too.' I remember because we both laughed. It was a power thing." Edie was not about to get into a rut she'd later regret, and Nelson once again plunged into a love affair in which he was the one to take out the garbage.

Still another man I talked to thought back to a woman he had dated a year earlier. "I love to stay in bed really late on Sundays, sometimes all day. Eat breakfast, have coffee, read the paper." This was Tony's way of relaxing, whether he was with a woman or alone. "This girl— Carey—always seemed to enjoy it, too, for about six months. Then all of a sudden (we were practically living together by then) she began to get up early on Sundays. She said she hated hanging around all day. Other little things changed, too. I felt as if she'd been lying all that time, like faking orgasms or something."

I doubt that Carey willfully lied about how she liked to spend her Sundays. Possibly she had enjoyed the novelty of those first months of lazy Sundays and only later, once the romance had settled in, so to speak, did she miss her own Sunday rituals. Perhaps she was trying too hard to be what Nelson wanted her to be. Even so, had she been more careful about conveying who she was (in this case, an enthusiastic morning person) from day one, Sunday mornings might never have become an issue.

I have no way of knowing for sure, but my sneaking suspicion is that women are generally more compliant than men at the beginning of a love affair. Even in this day and age, many of us have been brought up as nurturers, which in its worst sense means that we put our own needs and wishes behind those of others, and often at our own expense. True, many people (of all sexual persuasions) are generous and easygoing by nature. But a woman whose will to give consistently overshadows her will to take or even to ask for, or who chooses men with wills of unbendable steel, may be in a state of emotional detente, headed for all-out emotional war. One day, invariably, her will to be herself will supersede her will to be agreeable. We've all seen this in action: the woman who, after twenty years of marriage, explodes one night, enraged that "we always spend Saturday night with Leo and Brooke. I *hate* Leo and Brooke." Another woman, two years into a relationship, cries out, seemingly out of the blue, "We always stay at your place. Why can't you come schlepping over to my house once in a while?" or, "Make the bed yourself." Another woman might not be able to pinpoint the source of her frustration so easily and will simply burst into tears one day because she doesn't know if she can go on anymore "this way."

Man or woman, in the beginning of a love affair it's easy to forget who you are. Early love is not unlike a trance, where the easiest and possibly most pleasurable way to act for the moment is just to let it happen, as the saying goes. But the trouble with letting love happen is that if you're not there from the beginning—there as yourself—you'll end up as a character in somebody else's love affair, a case of mistaken identity. You don't want to lose yourself in love; you want to *find* yourself. So it's important, even in the illusory flush of a honeymoon, to own up to yourself and what matters to you, to remember who you are—and to let your lover in on the secret as well.

It's a point of etiquette to be truthful about yourself from the beginning. Honesty about small matters (no matter how much of a hurry you're in, you can't really figure out the larger issues this soon) will save confusion and hurt feelings later. Say so now if Indian food gives you hives; MSG, headaches; or French food, cellulite. Admit that you don't like to go shopping for someone else's clothes, to do drugs all the time or to jog at five in the morning. Speak up about what you'd like to do on the weekend, or whom you'd like to see. Yes, you can start over with a new lover—but only in some ways. And yes, you'll have to compromise a million times throughout a love affair—but not every compromise should be

yours. You owe it to yourselves and your future to establish ground rules that will make you both happy, now
and later. Not many real love affairs have come to an
early end because one or the other couldn't get to like
curry.

Okay, you've got certain things out in the open. You're
being as honest as you know how. You're adjusting to
each other's likes and dislikes. You're sitting in a dimly
lit restaurant, holding hands across a sticky, varnished
tabletop, drinking red wine and happily eating grilled-
cheese sandwiches and French fries, which you both happen to like. You're exchanging childhoods and early infatuations, telling stories in which you're the good guy and
even, if you really trust each other, in which you might
not have been. Your first private joke is a milestone.
You're beginning to get some ideas about what makes
this person, your lover, tick. You're endlessly curious
about what's going to happen to the two of you—but a
little too shy or too uncertain to bring it up. So for the
time being you put into sex the emotions and hopes you
can't yet put into words. Given half a chance, honeymoon
sex can be exalted. But sometimes, alas, real down-home
lovemaking gets lost in the zealous pursuit of sexual ac-
robatics.

The problem with sex lately is much like the problem
with Wonder Bread: It may help build strong bodies
twelve ways, but it's been so refined that the taste, texture
and earthiness suffer.

Earlier in this century we began to think seriously about
sex and science in the same breath; if science could bring
us Wonder Bread then, by golly, think what it could do
for sex. Freud is the most famous modern expert to try
to put sex into a scientific context, but hung up as he
was on parents, hysteria, cocaine and vaginal orgasms,

even he finally took the easy way out: "However strange it may sound, I think the possibility must be considered that something in the nature of sexual instinct itself is unfavorable to the achievement of absolute gratification." And there the subject rested for awhile until in the early Fifties Kinsey (who was, by the way, an expert on *wasps* before he became a sex expert) explained that no matter how up to date we thought ourselves, we were in fact sexually discontent, perhaps terminally so. The matter was urgent. When I was a little kid in the Fifties, I remember the grownups talking about Kinsey in the same nervous tones they used for Khrushchev and the Cold War. And thus sex therapy was invented.

I don't mean to imply that sex therapy is useless. Certainly "sexology" has done much to help us understand sexuality, and no doubt its techniques can help some people, some of the time. But could all of us really be so disturbed and ungratified? Mostly I object to sexology because it's gone too far: I'm suspicious of *any* institution that dehumanizes two people in love by calling them the "unit," and that lays out programs for improving "performance" so specific that they leave no room for laughter. What we've been looking for all along, I would think, is a more lyrical way to express ourselves in bed, the kind of sex that poets—not scientists—have always dreamed about. High-tech sex hasn't turned out to be the panacea we had hoped for; if it had, sex therapists, especially those whose training is dubious and who continually invent new sex problems (like whether or not there is such a thing as the G-spot) to keep us worried and themselves in business, wouldn't be multiplying like fruit flies. I personally have to go along with what one of Jules Feiffer's recent cartoon characters believes: "To learn everything about sex is to know nothing about sex." Maybe it's time to go back to our bodies for some of the answers.

It's taken us centuries to recover—insofar as we have—from all the trouble with the Puritans, Victorians and so on, and to learn all over again that sex is not only procreational and to an extent mechanical but also teasing, loving, spontaneous, whimsical and spirited. The trouble with sexology is that, with its solemn airs and fancy jargon, it's really pretty puritanical and antiseptic itself.

I was charmed when I read a book called *The Kiss and Its History*, which was published almost a century ago and which, among other things, describes how kissing found its way into fashion. Early in the nineteenth century, for example, fashionable English women wore a small-brimmed hat known as the "kiss me quick," which the Victorians characteristically replaced with a wide-brimmed affair, difficult to penetrate, called the "kiss me if you can" (a hat that you wore above the "touch me not" crinoline). When your mind is concentrated on making love (as human minds very often are) our hats, our gestures, everything we say and do becomes sexual. A sexually aware man or woman will pay attention to these cues. And there are simpler ways to celebrate sex than by memorizing instruction manuals.

Learning sex is like learning a language—French, let's say. And the object is to become so proficient in sex, as one would become in French, that you come to speak it without having to translate in your head, so that your gestures and words aren't studied but natural. So much of sex is instinct; your senses, if you put down your books and listen to them, will point you in the right direction. Everyone knows about the seductive power of soothing voices, the right music and soft lighting, and no one would argue that a little champagne can go a long way. Most of us know by instinct, too, that the sense of smell plays a part in sexuality—male rabbits whose olfactory glands are removed become impotent. Like people of all cultures we're great believers in colognes, powders and lotions—for both sexes—all of which, finally, add up to sex. A director will tell his actors to "fill the stage" with their performance; the aim in sex is to fill the love affair with your body, with everything about you that makes you sensual. When it comes to sex, let your body be your guide. Use all your senses: You and your lover want to see, smell, hear each other—even your sense of taste is heightened.

Throughout history people of every culture (with the exception of the Puritans, who banned spices and any foods that "excited passion") have attached sexual myths to certain foods, and now even nutritionists are getting into the aphrodisiac act. The *Kama Sutra* promises that "a mixture of ghee, sugar, liquorice, mixed with equal quantities of the juice of fennel and milk drunk daily will guarantee the preservation of one's sexual powers well into old age." The book also suggests asparagus, which scientists today concede *is* a stimulant. Oysters, too, have long been considered an aphrodisiac; Casanova ate fifty of them every day for breakfast. As it turns out, oysters are full of zinc, which produces sperm, as well as other substances that regulate male and female energy levels. The American colonists used dandelion to treat impotence; dandelion is packed with Vitamin A. Truffles, caviar, artichokes: It makes perfect sense that pleasurable foods can bring about pleasurable sex.

So don't back away from what makes you feel sensual. Wear the clothes that make you feel manly or feminine; surprise each other from time to time with romantic dinners. Appreciate your lover's scents. Find music to remind you of each other; show up sometime with a good bottle of wine and two antique wineglasses. Give sex a chance.

A book called *Bed Manners*, published some fifty years ago, claimed to be the first book about bedroom etiquette. By our standards it's pretty chaste stuff; married couples in twin beds; who should get up to chase flies at night; who should get up for burglars (nobody). But it makes the point that, "It is quite easy to show good manners while you are vertical. This is the normal position when taking off your hat to a lady, or selling her a bottle of gin in a store, or any other civilized action. When you assume a horizontal position, however, whole centuries of traditional good breeding disappear." The authors go on to discuss the proper atmosphere for the bedroom (e.g., "The presence of servants in the bedroom is absolutely okay at all times."). Still, behind the joking, the book does bring up some of the common bedroom hostilities—and argues that with a little courtesy on all sides they're avoidable.

Lovers, too, have to create the proper atmosphere for the bedroom. It's important for each of you to feel at home in the other's bedroom, and not as if you're the outsider. The cleaner, fresher and more welcoming a bedroom is, the more open you'll feel about sex. A surplus of your clothing or clutter all over the place, too many mementoes of this lover or that wife, even too much evidence of your children, can be disheartening to your lover. A man I interviewed complained that twice when he went to sit down on his friend's bed (she was a painter) he found that he had sat on her artist's palette. A woman in her late twenties felt stifled by her lover's daughter: "He has a daughter. I don't really mind, and I couldn't do anything about it anyway. But his bedroom is like a shrine to her: a portrait over the bed, pictures along one wall, on the night table. It's more *her* bedroom than anyone else's."

Once you're sleeping with someone regularly each of you has a stake in the other's life. Like it or not, falling in love means that sooner or later you'll have to make subtle changes in your life and surroundings to allow room for your friend. Later we'll get to the "ceremony" of giving up a drawer to a lover, but for now it's good manners to assure your friend with small gestures that he or she is a "presence" in your life. Maybe your friend would appreciate the suggestion that he or she leave a pair of jeans at your house, or you might buy something personal, a T-shirt or a razor, "for you to use when you're here." Keep in stock the things he or she likes to eat and drink. Such small subtleties make a difference. I remember when a friend and I took up a word game called Boggle. We had a set at his house, and another at mine. Whenever I saw the Boggle game on the shelf in his living room I felt welcome, connected to him; I imagine he felt the same way about the game at my house. (Later, of course, I wanted to break the Boggle game over his head, but that's hardly the point.)

What so many of us fear most, it seems to me, is the one false move that, even at this still relatively early stage, could show we care enough to be hurt, that we're vulnerable to having a lover say: "You'd better go now, and be sure to take that extra pair of jeans with you." Most human beings aren't as cruel as we imagine, however, and nobody worth knowing is going to ridicule you for making the first gesture toward emotional attachment. ("And then she said—do you believe this?—that I could leave a pair of jeans at her house if I wanted!") It's more likely that when it comes time to talk about "what all this means" you'll each remember with gratitude the efforts the other has made, and you'll both feel more trusting. You'll also feel gratified to know, whether or not the affair works out the way you want it to in the long run, that you gave what you could. As far as sex is concerned, you'll be more relaxed and willing about it if you're certain from the beginning that you matter in your friend's life.

Both the men and the women I talked to deeply resent the sense one sometimes has that one of you is falling in love while the other is thinking simply of having a good time. If you're together on the honeymoon, there's never a better time to be open and eager about sex, to be willing to try new things and to talk about sex.

As for being open and eager about sex, that's usually not a problem at the beginning, when sex is both brand new and becoming almost familiar. Usually it's more a problem at this stage to remember to go to work, eat dinner or show up at your family reunion than it is to remember to make love. Chances are good that trying new things won't be a problem, either. You'll almost *have* to try new things, spending all that time in bed. But as for talking about sex, that's something else again.

With all the talk about talking about sex, it's still not easy for many of us to say, "Hey, remember last night when we...." When I think of bringing the subject up I think of what it was like for a Victorian woman to go to the doctor. The doctor would hold up a dummy shaped more or less like a human being and the woman, who was accompanied by either her mother or her husband, would point mutely to the area that ailed her, which the doctor then examined as well as he could, while the patient remained fully dressed. Victorian men may have had an easier time at the doctor's than Victorian women, but it's no easier now for nervous men to talk about sex than it is for nervous women. And there are a lot of nervous types out there.

But it's not so hard to talk about sex as all that. The first rule comes from the sex therapists, who rightly feel that it's better not to talk about sexual problems or difficulties when you're in bed; even a football coach waits until his team gets back to the locker room before he bawls the players out. The caring lover, one who is hopeful that this affair will continue to grow, will be gentle about starting the sexual discourse. It's wise, for example, not to talk about what's *wrong* with sex between you before you've had many happy discussions about what's *good* about it. You don't to start a lifelong pattern where you both turn rigidly defensive at the very mention of sex. If you can't stand that after six weeks your lover has not yet got around to Position Seventy-four, The Approach from the Window, don't let your unhappiness become the occasion for the first sexual conversation you have. It won't kill you to wait a week or two for that. Practice makes perfect, after all, and good sex takes time and practice.

Sexual discussions don't have to be deep and philosophical, either. You can say, "Let's talk about sex," in a playful way over dinner, riding bikes, during a tickling match. Practice that way first. The point is that sex should be as easy a subject for conversation as the weather (it's certainly less boring), and not something that comes up only when there's a problem. If the subject makes you queasy, or if you hate sounding clinical about it, put your questions not in a technical way but romantically. "Did you have the multiple orgasm you were anticipating, my dear?" could be re-phrased: "Tell me what it feels like when you come," and then, "Do you feel that with me?" Instead of saying, "Do you find the way I perform fellatio to your satisfaction?" you can bring the subject up gradually: "What do you like best about sex?" "Do you like this?" "This?"

Learn to talk about sex in an abstract way, too, to find out how your lover feels about this or that. "There's an article in the paper today about trampoline sex. I'd never heard of that before." And there you'll be, talking about trampoline sex. Or, "A friend of a friend of a friend of Martha's is taking a course in Advanced Foreplay 306.

Don't you think that's going a little too far?" If you don't know how to bring up a subject that might be hurtful in a circuitous way, or if you prefer to be direct, remember that all of us, men, women, even eunuchs, have sexual egos that are easily bruised. "Don't you know, Blanche, that the missionary position went out with the missionaries?" is not going to make Blanche feel very good. And Rudolph can't be blamed for his actions if you say, "Did you know, Rudolph, that you don't always have to wait til it's dark?" Possibly you could begin by saying, "I love it when you..." and then suggest that, "Maybe we could...."

A marriage manual considered particularly racy when it was first published in 1951 warned that petting between young unmarried people, if not controlled, could turn into a habit, like marijuana, which was supposed to head you straight to heroin. As courting adults that's exactly what we want: to make sexuality a habit. If you're wholeheartedly addicted to someone, you'll notice how sex changes as your love grows, from insatiably passionate to romantically hopeful and finally to the unquestioning sex that confirms a deep love. This, of course, is sex that renews itself through the kind of love one dreams about. And if you can give yourself during your honeymoon you're part way there.

The temptation during the honeymoon is to do what many people do when a suspense novel begins to get scary: flip to the last few pages, skipping over the heart of the book to see what will happen in the end. You can do it if you must with a thriller, but no matter how eager and frightened you are, there's no way to do it in a love affair. Still, it's baffling at times when sexual attachment precedes emotional involvement. As psychotherapist Rollo May wrote in *Love and Will*:

> It is a strange thing in our society that what goes into building a relationship—the sharing of tastes, fantasies, dreams, hopes for the future, and fears from the past—seems to make more people shy and vulnerable than going to bed with each other. They are more wary of the tenderness that goes with psychological and spiritual nakedness than they are of the physical nakedness in sexual intimacy.

Yes, I think most of us are more afraid of emotional nakedness than we are of sex, but as often as this question comes up I'm still not sure that the problem is all that special. People were terrified of sex back in the days when emotional intimacy preceded lovemaking. It's natural to be jittery about what's coming next.

Even so, the honeymoon *can* be frightening: You're offering up your heart without receiving any promises in return. That's a real departure from our courtship tradition, a tradition that has always meant promises. For your part, you may be making silent promises left and right, but who's to say that what you want, what you're promising yourself, is going to match up with what your friend wants? You know perfectly well that one, maybe both of you, could get hurt.

In most adult love affairs, there are plenty of outside circumstances to cloud the happiness of a honeymoon: an old lover or wife or husband lurking nearby; the reluctance of your lover "to get involved"; a difference in age; an impending transfer to Seattle; the complications of children; conflicts of race, professional liaisons, religion, money. And, depressingly, on and on.

Yet we do, of course, go on, intrepid seekers of love that we are. And with all the risks of taking on a lover—having your heart broken; being party to adultery when you may not even have known that that nice girl whose eyes crinkled when she smiled was married to a jealous, weight-lifting lawyer; falling in love with a kleptomaniac; catching crabs—most of us would rather take the chance than not.

You're admitting that you'd rather take the chance when you come as far as the honeymoon. There are variations, of course; no love affair operates strictly according to the book (even according to *this* book). Some people plunge right into a relationship, skipping the honeymoon stage for now, and introducing a lover to friends right away ("I couldn't fall in love with someone who didn't get along with my friends."); others, ever hopeful, rearrange their lives at the first hint of love. But whatever the schedule, what each of us wants to do as soon as we can is, in the words of the Fleetwood Mac song, to "wrap around" someone's dreams. It's not a bad thing to want to do.

Your courtship will progress as it progresses, however, and no faster. There's no cheating, no looking ahead to see what's going to happen. But once you're lovers, once you've come this far, you won't be able to put the book down until you've read it all the way through, through chapters that get even scarier and more suspenseful.

This is the point where your love affair is setting its own pace. Let it do that for a while. Don't fall into the trap that one of writer Richard Yates's characters came to regret: "All his life, it seemed, he had spoiled things for himself by worrying too soon." We'll get to worrying later, and then you can worry all you want. Meantime, as a writer from the last century advised in a guide for the "modern man and maid": "The touch of sentiment may be an indication of promising possibilities, but we should not take [it] on a single indication; we should await developments."

Chapter Eight

Settling In

WE WESTERNERS love a good romance. And in a good romance, as we define it, the lovers have countless adventures and must make their way against staggering odds before they can even begin to think about living happily ever after. We don't quite trust a romance that does not have its built-in obstacles, or one that does not create them along the way—that is to say, a love that runs too smoothly. Instead, we expect passion to be accompanied by torment and tears, as it usually is in a good movie.

Creating obstacles, however, is almost never the problem in grown-up relations.

It's when the honeymoon is over, when the pitch of your feelings has fallen an octave, that you really begin to look around and ask yourself, "What's going on here, anyway?" The qualities in your lover that please you may not have diminished at all, but for the first time in ages you remember that you have all the other parts of your life to think of, and notice that you've been thrown a little off balance by the surprise of this affair. You begin to wonder how this person will fit into the larger scheme of your life: whether he or she will get along with your friends and family, what part you'll play in your friend's life, where you'll be in six months or a year, whether you both have the same hopes, more or less, for the future. Reality, in short, sets in. And happily-ever-afterhood may suddenly seem a long way off.

At this point, most of us run through a brief analysis of the situation:

What am I doing here? This woman is an Italian who hardly speaks English and earns her living doing voice-overs for pasta commercials. I don't even speak Italian.

What am I doing here? This guy works the night shift for the CIA, and yesterday I caught him going through my briefcase.

What am I doing here? I'm going to be forty-six; this girl's twenty-four. The other night she had to explain that Blondie's not married to Dagwood Bumstead but a rock group. She thinks the Beatles were what Paul McCartney did before Wings.

You might be troubled by his four previous marriages, her eight kids, his vasectomy or her job as a stewardess for Air Mongolia. It might bother you that you work together, that she's Catholic and you're Jewish, that he's black and you're white, that she's not divorced yet, that he used to go out (last week) with your best friend, that she's lonely for her family in South Dakota, that he looks more longingly at your brother than he does at you, that she likes the *Today Show* and you watch *Good Morning America*. You might be a Republican, she a Democrat. For all the affection you feel, you may begin to think that there's little hope. You may be right.

In traditional courtship there was always a moment when the newness wore off: Everyone was allowed to relax a bit. Mom and Dad knew the young man or woman in question, and anyone concerned had a pretty good idea where the romance was headed. The young woman began to air the carefully stored linens in her hope chest. And the young man, sex on his mind, could see that to get what he wanted he'd have to follow the rules. In all probability the story would have the usual ending; it was only a question of time until Mr. and Mrs. Smugnose had the pleasure of requesting your presence at the marriage of their daughter Florette to Upright Dunkirk III. Meantime, Florette and Upright were allowed a few walks in the garden or an unchaperoned carriage ride so that they could stare yearningly into each other's eyes, and be in love.

While Florette and Upright might by now have wanted nothing more than a few minutes away from their beaming elders, we, at a comparable stage, have probably had quite enough of each other alone and may want nothing more than a little outside diversion, a break from the honeymoon. This is a turning point for us, too: We're about to see whether anything else about us fits together as well as our bodies do.

At this point in courtship a lot of players drop out. By the time you have your first "serious talk" it might become clear to you both that what each of you wants is so incongruous that the affair has no chance of going further. One of you may be willing to work at love while the other isn't. Perhaps you'll move from being lovers to being friends as easily as some people go from being friends to being lovers. A change in one life—let's say she finally gets her law degree and feels suddenly stronger, more independent—may cause such an upheaval in the way your relationship previously worked that neither of you can adjust to the pressure of new circumstances. Possibly the "honeymoon" has gone on so long with no signs of becoming something more that one of you becomes frustrated or bored. Maybe the obstacles would be too awesome even for a good movie. Looking back on my own history, I can see now, although I surely couldn't understand this at the time, that a number of relationships that mattered to me drew to their natural close at this point—just when both of us had to decide whether to become serious or not—and only much later did I understand why they couldn't have continued beyond the honeymoon.

On the other hand, you might, after appraising the pros and cons, want to explore this love affair further; the future might not seem unconquerable to you: You may *know* that this is what you want or, more likely, you may know that this is what you *might* want. Nicolette Larson sings a song that begins, "It's gonna take a lot of love to change the way things are." That's what you're hoping: that there will be enough love between you to make all the risks worthwhile. You're in for the duration.

A while back I was heading out with my tape recorder several evenings a week to talk to people about courtship. My habit was to play the tapes back on Saturdays, transcribing the passages I wanted to keep. During one of the playback sessions, I listened to four tapes, two men and two women, and heard four uncannily identical complaints: "Women always want a commitment right away...." "The women are unbelievable. They always want to get involved too fast...." "Men start planning your future the minute they get you into bed...." "I don't know. These guys just want to settle down right away." Maybe I should have called all four of them right then and there to arrange a meeting.

Obviously the problem isn't that everyone wants to get involved too soon; if that were the case there wouldn't be a problem and no one would ever be alone. The trouble, instead, is that some people want to get involved faster than others, and unfortunately there's usually one of each sort in every relationship. Because this issue is so telling, so important, one way or another, to most men and women, the "speed limit" for a relationship is often the first deeply personal question to arise as a romance begins to get serious.

Early in a love affair you'll willingly give up a certain amount of privacy, and put off asking some of the questions you'd like to ask, in order to attend to a new and fragile intimacy. Sooner or later, however, you'll want to begin comparing emotional needs. You'll be itchy to talk about the future, or you'll be itchy *not* to talk about the future—two sides of the same coin. Like an inept detective, you'll begin to draw conclusions about things that engage your curiosity but that you can't bring yourself to talk about: "He said he's going to the hockey game with some friends tonight. Obviously he's seeing his old girlfriend." Or, "She said that kid who threw chow mein at his mother in the restaurant was disgusting. Clearly she doesn't like children."

Bit by bit, you'll gather these pieces of "evidence" together, as you begin to fill in the picture of your partner. Using what you know, you will find as you grow closer endless new questions to negotiate: How much time will you spend together? How often will you call each other? In how much detail will you be asked to account for your time apart? What about fidelity? the future? How would your friend react if you simply turned up at his or her apartment late one night? or if you called up, because you were lonely, at three in the morning? In other words, just where do you stand?

A reasonable question. And the obvious strategy here is to take the bull by the horns and ask, "Hey, just where do we stand?" But this direct approach, a strategy invented by someone with a tin ear for love, ignores centuries of courtship wisdom. The direct approach does not work, never has. Courtship at this stage has to be treated delicately, like a heart transplant. Nobody in his or her right mind will ever answer, "You're right. We've known each other for two months now and it's time for a plan. Let's spend the rest of our lives together." Much as you want to, insisting on a plan now is probably bad manners for at least two reasons: first, you're likely to start a needless argument; and second, you're asking, or forcing, your friend to invent pipe dreams about the future or simply to lie.

Human beings have an amazing compulsion to try to predict and control the future. Everyone from economists ("The recession will be over in sixty-seven days") to investors ("I'll take the pork-belly futures") to weathermen ("The fourth of July will be sunny and warm") tries his hand at the future, often with results no more accurate than what a pack of tarot cards would have produced. When the future rests on something as immediate as your love life, the compulsion to predict can get out of hand. So relax. It's impossible to predict or control what you'll do next week, let alone for the rest of your life, if your plans depend on what someone else wants to do, particularly when that someone else isn't talking.

You may know all about Clyde's darkest secret—that he broke his mother's favorite vase when he was seven, blamed it on the maid and to this day hasn't told the truth about it—yet you're afraid to invite him to Cousin Shelby's wedding next month, for fear he might tell you that he doesn't want to plan that far ahead. But then you remember the time he said, "Maybe we'll go to Greece next summer." Why did that seem so unreal to you? Could next summer really be so far away?

Most of us can put our energy to better use than by trying to second-guess the future. There are ways around asking the big questions that will teach you all sorts of things about your lover, your future, even yourself, without bringing up issues that neither of you can really decide now. You have a lot more evidence to gather before you can figure out whether this relationship will suit you over the long haul, let alone whether it will suit your friend. After all, you've been living on your honeymoon; you really don't know the first thing about each other's lives. As for the future, it has a way of figuring itself out. Where love is concerned, there's only so much you can do to help it along. So concentrate for now on the questions that *can* be answered. Meanwhile, if you *must* ask the big questions, take five dollars and go ask your local palm reader.

If you want to know what your lover means by "relationship," the first thing you'll have to learn, curiously enough, is how he or she defines privacy. You can't build a life together until you understand how you conduct your lives separately. We're not talking about the "boys' night out" kind of privacy: What you have to figure out instead is where the "empty spaces" are in your friend's life and whether you can fill them. You have to figure out, too, whether you have the same empty spaces—and whether your lover is capable of filling up *yours*.

As a general rule, I've discovered, one person's idea of a relationship is another person's idea of strangulation.

Perhaps you envision a love affair where you'll spend all your spare moments together, while your lover prefers to spend a good deal of time alone or doing other things that don't involve you, whether he or she is in love or not. There is no question of right or wrong here; you simply have different ideas about relationships, about privacy, about how you want your lives to work. This doesn't mean you're at an impasse or that you'll never sort things out, only that you're about to discover how intimate, according to your lover, intimate really *is*. You will also discover how to be generous about seeing to your lover's "empty spaces," and how willing he or she will be to see to yours.

Many of us adults are accustomed to being alone much of the time, and as a result have come to be fairly self-reliant. Falling in love disrupts this solitude, and we take a while to adjust to sharing time and territory, even with someone we love. Maybe if we had fallen in love irrevocably when we were younger, as Florette Smugnose and Upright Dunkirk III did a couple of generations back, we wouldn't now be so fixed in our habits. But we didn't, and the privacy we've by now come to appreciate seems essential to maintaining personal equilibrium. Many people complained to me that they felt their privacy was invaded each time they fell in love. Others admitted they felt "jealous" when a lover wanted to go off alone or when a lover's life seemed fuller to begin with than theirs. If you can, save your jealousy for occasions when you have real cause to be self-righteous and indignant. Privacy can be negotiated again at each stage. For now, as you learn more about each other, it's wise to keep a respectful distance.

For example, I know a man who likes to spend each Thursday night alone, regardless of the state of his love life. He's social on the weekends, and he uses Thursdays to tend to his personal chores. A woman falling in love with him could jump to any number of conclusions about this ritual: He doesn't need me on Thursdays; He's doing something else on Thursdays; He's doing something he doesn't want me to know about on Thursdays; He's cheating on Thursdays and lying about it on Fridays— so what good is he the rest of the week? By the weekend she'd be a wreck. If, on the other hand, she had taken the time to understand what his life was like before she decided to change it, she would have seen that Thursdays were no threat to her. Thursdays, in fact, have nothing to do with her. She would have understood that part of his idea of intimacy is his need for breathing space at the rate of one healthy breath each Thursday.

I remember a man I went out with for a while who was eager for us to spend as much time together as we could. His attention was flattering, but at times overwhelming. "Well, if you can't see me, what are you going to do tonight?" he asked one day. "I don't know, read a little, do some laundry maybe, just hang around. I've got lots of little things to do," I told him. I did have plenty to do; I also needed some time to be alone. But the fact that I wouldn't see him, that the laundry came first, was too much for him. Other times, though, I've been just as devastated by someone else's wish to be alone. There are many times in love when you'll have to barge unceremoniously into your dear one's privacy, just as there are times when the best thing to do is embrace your autonomy and go off to do your own laundry. The point is to be able to intuit the difference.

There are other, more complicated ways to invade privacy. One such invader was a man who, without warning, decided to surprise his friend by picking her up at her exercise class. Toward the end of her workout, she glanced up and saw him in the anteroom. As she describes it, "I looked like a whale in a leotard trying to pretend to be Jane Fonda. When I saw him he waved. Waved! I wanted to kill him. You don't just show up somewhere like that."

Meanwhile, in a love affair across town, another man accused both his lover and his secretary of invasion of privacy. The woman he was seeing was in the natural habit of calling his office from time to time, and struck up a casual friendship with his secretary. He began to notice a new familiarity on his secretary's part: She would ask, for instance, how such-and-such a restaurant had been the night before, or even whether he was feeling less cranky than he had felt over the weekend. His girlfriend, too, began to intrude on his office life: "How was that meeting with the electric shoehorn account?" His office life and his personal life, lives which he had always taken pains to keep separate, closed in on him. "A triangle with my girlfriend and my secretary," he said, "that's crazy. I feel like everyone's ganging up on me."

Confusion also arises when one person's idea of "natural curiosity" is the other's idea of invasion of privacy. One woman, for example, got home late several nights in one week and found the phone ringing—it was her boy friend each time—when she walked in the door. "He was checking up on me," she complained. "I had promised that I'd call him when I got in."

"Natural curiosity" was the bone of contention in another relationship in which a man had started seeing a woman he liked, although his previous affair, while coming to an end, was not completely over yet. He had asked the second woman, his new friend, to be patient, promising that he'd end the first relationship completely as soon as he felt he could. She wouldn't take him at his word: "She asks me about it every day.... 'Did you tell her yet?' These things take time and I don't need any more pressure about it. Also, it's none of her business, really, and I don't think I should have to fill her in on all the details."

Other people I talked to complained about a lover flipping through the mail ("She was just glancing at the bills, not even doing it in secret"), asking who called every time the phone rang ("He always says, 'Who was that?' and pretends to be casual about it") or invading privacy in more traditional ways, such as assuming joint bathroom rights. To some people, even the question, "What did you do last night?" is loaded. It seems that we're all pretty idiosyncratic about when we want to be left alone and when we don't, or about how much of our lives we're willing to share.

Where privacy is concerned, the rule should be that neither side should assume too much, or too soon. For example, don't assume that love means never having to say "May I?" Your rights as a lover, at least early on, are only those that have been accorded you. And don't assume that you're necessarily entitled to the rights you're prepared to give your lover—that's coercion.

Meanwhile, don't go too far the other way and presume that your lover will pick up through osmosis what *you* mean by privacy. Many men, although I can't for the life of me figure out why, get all worked up when a woman borrows a razor. But unless she's told, how is she to know that her male friend, who on all other counts might be perfectly reasonable, will fly into an inhuman rage if she borrows his razor to use on her dainty legs? Or how is a man to know that a woman resents surprise visits, that she'd prefer a call first? Or that her address book is off limits, even to her lover?

The boundaries of love are like expanding concentric circles. Your feelings for each other at first form a tiny common circle, then a slightly bigger one outside the first, then a bigger one still. You'll take turns inviting each other from circle to circle, and sometimes you'll know that you're welcome in the next circle even if you're not formally invited. Each time you move from one circle to the next you'll be a little closer to each other—and you'll give up a little more of your privacy, a few more of your secrets. But circle-hopping takes time. It's something that's not easy for many of us. The thoughtful lover will adjust his or her speed, sometimes speeding up and other times slowing down, so that you both can cross the boundaries together.

To excel at love while you're still in the early stages you'll not only have to be a mind reader about privacy; you'll also have to be an expert at translating what your lover says into what he or she really means. Reading between the lines of love is a sensitive art.

As we've seen, courtship once had a comprehensible set of guidelines: Here's what you do first, here's how to keep the thing going, here's what happens in the end. All the lines were written in advance. Even love letters followed a specific format, laid out in how-to books on love. One such book published in the last century, *Ready-Made Love Letters*, had a letter for every imaginable occasion, one hundred thirty-four of them in all. For example:

Letter 119—From a Young Lady to a Gentleman, Complaining of Indifference
Letter 120—The Gentleman's Answer
Letter 121—From a Gentleman to a Lady Whom He Accuses of Inconstancy
Letter 122—From a Lady to a Lover who Suspects her of Receiving the Addresses of Another~In Answer

And so on. The book also includes five all-purpose
"specimen" love letters. In those days an entire courtship
could be pursued literally by the same book. The point
was for these earlier lovers to know exactly where they
stood at any moment of their courtship.

Part of the game, too, was strategy. Everyone knew
that, among her other ruses, the young woman had to
play hard to get from time to time. How else would she
keep a young man on his toes? Another etiquette book
of the last century, *Young Lady's Friend*, outlined the
strategy in no uncertain terms:

> If one person is becoming uppermost in your
> thoughts, if his society is more and more necessary
> to your happiness, if what he does and says seems
> more important than that of anyone else, it is time
> to be on your guard, time to deny yourself the dan-
> gerous pleasure of his company, time to turn your
> thoughts resolutely to something else.

Your move, sir. The young man, of course, had his re-
course: he had also picked up the rules and strategies of
the game. And in *The Fusser's Book: Rules by Anna Archbald*, he was warned:

> Remember that all that chills you is not cold. In all
> probability she has been advised to refuse an invi-

tation once in awhile, or to be out occasionally when you call. Above all she may fear to give the impression that she is sitting at the telephone waiting for you to ring her up. Learn to distinguish between a slight frost and the cold spell that ushers in a whole winter of discontent.

Even as recently as during the first days of the telephone, the last thing ladies and gentlemen were permitted to do was reveal their true feelings. Etiquette books disciplined lovers relentlessly. "Be a little cruel; not always nice. He will like you better," one such book advised the lady. But the man didn't have to take this treatment passively: "Suggest that 'it's all off' even if you intend calling her on the 'phone within the hour. This tactic adds the two ingratiating elements of elusiveness and surprise to your intercourse."

Back then, the games people played were considered a good thing. They were right out in the open: Everyone played more or less the same games, knew all the rules, even knew the outcome in advance. If everything else was on course, the games merely added a little whimsy and intrigue to the courtship. But all that has changed. Games are now said to be a *bad* thing. We don't acknowledge them; we don't learn the rules. Instead, you're supposed to say what you mean and mean what you say.

In fact it's not possible to be so up front about your feelings all the time—in love, marriage, friendship or even, I suppose, in therapy. Sometimes we have to play games. You can't say to your boss, "You know, this company would be better off if you worked for *me* instead of the other way around," nor could you say to a close friend, "That dress you saved up for all summer makes you look like an eggplant." And we also have to be discreet at times about our feelings in love. Some games are perfectly natural, even desirable, in courtship—even rabbits know how to be coy. When the male rabbit is ready to make love, the female, if she's following proper rabbit etiquette, will suddenly feign indifference at the last minute, leaving him stunned while she goes off to look for something to eat. And so the chase begins all over again.

Our problem today is that we no longer know how to play our own games by the rules—but that does not mean that our courtship is more straightforward than it was for Florette and Upright. Traditional courtship, with all its games and rules, was actually more explicit. The problem for us is that we're each playing different games according to rules that we ourselves have devised. Often in the midst of a love affair we feel lonely and uncertain, wondering where love will "take" us and feeling as if no one has ever gone through a romance in quite this way before. And so we're more confused than ever.

The man who said to a woman a century ago, "You're the most beautiful woman I've ever seen," was speaking in a code they both understood. They knew he was playing a game. What he meant was that she was beautiful enough for him and that he was willing to give up all others for her. But today the code is unclear and leads to misunderstanding. A man who says that to a woman now arouses her suspicion. "Aha," she might reply, "what are you *really* saying? Your ex-wife, after all, was elected queen of the computer-chip festival, and your old girl friend was a model." She's taking his words at face value. What she's saying to herself is, "I'm *not* the most beautiful woman he's ever seen; perhaps he thinks I'm ugly." She doesn't know his code; she hasn't learned the game.

Because the language of love is a language unto itself, you can't rely on your grasp of basic English to get by. You'll have to learn in each case to translate everyday English into the various dialects of love. And while each of us transmits a code that's unique, there are a few elements common to most. Remembering these will help crack even the most mysterious or ambiguous signals.

The first rule of code-breaking is that you cannot always hold someone responsible for a statement made in the heat of emotion. The *Oxford English Dictionary* defines emotion as: "any agitation or disturbance of mind, feeling, passion; any vehement or excited mental state." From this it's clear that people in love act much the way crazy people do. One can't always hold crazy people responsible for irrational behavior; we should give people in love the same leeway.

A woman I interviewed some months back was distraught over the "mixed signals" she was receiving from her lover. "One time he got all excited about a house for rent he heard about," she said. "We hadn't even been going out for that long. But it was a really good deal and he thought maybe we should just take it and take a chance living together." The deal came and went. A few months later she herself brought up the subject of living together. "He said he couldn't live with anybody. He wasn't ready for that. But sometimes he says, 'When we live together it'll be really nice,' things like that. I can't figure out what he's talking about."

Many of our codes give out conflicting messages of this kind. There are people who on the one hand will say something like, "My children need a father figure around the house," and on the other, "I'll never get married again after what I went through before." Some people will follow their statement that "I've never felt so close to anyone else" two minutes later with, "I'm not ready to be involved." Other codes involve promises: "I rented a ski house for the winter. You'll have to come up all the time." So you wax up your skis—only to dust them off, unused, when you notice the first spring tulips. Some people are madly affectionate one day, distant the next; others disappear for weeks at a time and then re-surface, acting as if no time at all has gone by. And some people will behave as if they're deliberately "testing" you—standing you up, breaking a date for no reason, forgetting to call as promised—checking, knowingly or unknowingly, to see how you'll respond.

Balzac said that in love "man is an orangutan with a violin." Women aren't necessarily any better. To decipher what your lover is trying to say behind the rhetoric of love you'll have to remind yourself how graceless we often are where our feelings are concerned. If on the first summer evening, after an elegant dinner in an outdoor café, a man says to a woman, "Let's elope to Paris," what is he really saying? Should she pack? Can she sue if he elopes to Paris the following week with someone else? What *can* you believe?

I recently had dinner with an old boyfriend, who was in town for a couple of days, and, as usual, the talk turned to the days when we had gone out together. I accused him (in the most polite way, to be sure) of being disingenuous when it came to love. Predictably, he was shocked; he felt that he wasn't disingenuous at all: "I meant everything I ever said to you. At least I meant it when I said it. I can't help it if things don't turn out the way they're supposed to."

I also talked about this disingenuousness in love with a woman I interviewed. "If I say I love someone," she said, "or that maybe things will work out, I'm usually feeling that way. But sometimes you say things to sort of try them out, to see how they sound." Voicing affection or making a promise is, then, in some of our codes, a way of acting on an impulse to make it seem real, perhaps because you'd *like* it to be real. Under a code like this, if I say everything will work out fine then maybe everything *will* work out fine.

It wasn't as easy in the days of *Ready-Made Love Letters* to "try on" promises and feelings in this way; back then, the promises of love were more like public announcements. Cynical as this may sound, when it comes to decoding what your lover has to say it's wise, I think, to keep in mind that actions finally speak louder than words. Falling in love sends you for a while into an exaggerated state of being; emotion is so fluid. Some days you'll feel so close; other days you'll be miles apart. And sometimes one of you will feel needy for the other—and the other will be oblivious to that need. What you have to find is the lifeline of affection that's always within reach, even in the most turbulent times. And you'll have to search deeper than your lover's words for that lifeline.

What your lover's code can tell you, though, is how she's been hurt, what his dreams are, what she's most afraid of, how much he wants to fall in love. If you surprise yourself by saying, after ten weeks, "When we get married, let's try to get a little place in the country," you're probably not—assuming you're a decent sort to begin with—leading your lover on, even if you have no intention of planning marriage at this point. The translation might be: "I've always wanted a little place in the country when I get married. It's this dream I have. How does that sound?"

The woman who says, "I don't want any commitments right now," might really be saying, "I want more than anything else to be involved with you." Or she might not. The man who says, "I want to be free to see other people, too," might really be saying, "I sense that I like you more than you like me. Would you be upset—as I hope you would be—if I were to see other people?" Or he might be saying something else entirely. Whatever the code, you'll have to be gentle about translating it: We all use words to build ourselves up or put ourselves down; to say who we are and who we'd like to be; to exaggerate and defend and even re-shape the truth a little. But everyone has such a code and behind every code is an agenda for love. If you care enough to figure it out, you'll have to distinguish among hope, fear and real feelings. You'll have to know when to let an outrageous statement slip by as if unnoticed, and when to challenge. You'll learn that the language of love is not to be trusted entirely, nor mistrusted entirely.

You'll also find that you're speaking in a code of your own. You're saying things like, "Oh, I forgot that we were supposed to get together last night, too," even though you hadn't forgotten at all. Or you'll agree that true love is impossible to sustain, just for the sake of agreeing with your recently divorced and cynical lover, even though you don't believe that for a minute. A danger to avoid, however, is making your own code too abstruse; the object is to have your feelings within reach, for someone who loves you to find.

Another danger is to keep to your code at the expense of good manners. When you're in love you can't always be yourself, or put yourself first. Sometimes you'll have to seem to be friendly when you're not feeling friendly at all; you'll have to listen when you don't feel like it; you'll have to be polite and congenial, even if it's more in your nature to be rude and antisocial. You'll have to make small talk when you'd rather be reading the newspaper in peace and quiet—or you'll have to take in stride that some people never learn to make small talk when they'd rather be reading the paper in peace and quiet. Such are the manners of love. Most people in love spend a lot of time asking themselves, "Who needs this aggravation?" before remembering that they're the ones in love; they're the ones who need it.

Most of us find, though, that all this is too much to learn by ourselves, no matter how good a student we might be. Love takes place in the real world, not in the cocoon in which it begins. Very likely what you want now is to go out and try your love in the world, to celebrate these feelings among your friends and perhaps your family, your children, simply to get away from emotional questions and have some fun. You've been talking about "this guy Robert" or "you know, Carolyn," for so long now that your friends are eager to meet him or her, or perhaps already feel acquainted. Your impulse now is to bring everyone together, to make a big new happy family. Or, as the saying goes, "The world is a wedding."

Chapter Nine

Friends and Relations

MY MOTHER still tells the story of the first time she met my father's parents, how nervous she felt having tea in their living room. Before my father could intervene, his mother asked the two to stay on and have dinner. Feeling as if the hour-long visit had already lasted a month, my mother politely said something like, "How nice. I'd love to, if you're sure it won't be any trouble." She and my father then had to squirm their way through an endless dinner, evading the questions my formidable grand-mother put to them, and wishing they were off drinking beer with their friends instead.

The nervousness she felt at that first meeting is familiar to most of us; it's the same nervousness we feel when we meet a lover's friends for the first time, the same eagerness to make a good impression. Going public—bringing our separate lives together—is as great a step today as going private was for our ancestors. What if Joe, who has known

Willy for fifteen years to your three months, pulls Willy aside while you're in the ladies' room to say, "Hey, Will, no offense but you can do better than this"? Possibly you're a little nervous, too, about introducing Willy to *your* friends. What if he doesn't like them and decides, as a result, that maybe you're a little peculiar too? What if they don't like him? What's more, there are so many people to draw into your courtship—his or her friends, and yours; the children, if either of you has any; your parents, step-parents, sisters, brothers, ex-in-laws, aunts, uncles, cousins and grandparents; your professional-social friends—that anywhere along the line, something could easily go wrong.

On my questionnaires, I asked when in a love affair one introduced a new lover to friends, and to the children and the rest of the crew. One response was fairly typical. A man of thirty wrote from Florida that he would get together with friends as soon as he felt certain he cared about a woman. Once he'd crossed that barrier, he'd introduce the woman to his young son. Finally she would meet his parents, "probably at the church on the way to the altar."

With our families far off or often not terribly involved in the day-to-day details of our lives, most of us adults rely on our friends for advice, support and companionship. So it's important to us that our friends approve of the lovers we choose. Sharing your lover with your friends is tantamount to giving a gift to both sides. You picture everyone getting along, expanding your social circle by one (like the old Farmer in the Dell game) and putting the pieces of your life together, but with an added dimension—your lover will be taking a rightful place alongside you.

In the days when meeting a lover's parents was the lovers' debut, so to speak, the natural distance between parents and offspring served to give such meetings a certain degree of formality. To your lover's parents you'd talk about your family or your plans; or you'd chat about the weather. Mainly you wanted to appear presentable. Generally you knew ahead of time what to worry about (wrong religion, wrong social class, wrong job, wrong character, that tattoo). You could anticipate the objections and plan for the counterattack. *Guess Who's Coming to Dinner?* notwithstanding, chances were good that you'd pass the parent test or you wouldn't have been invited in the first place. Parents, after all, are usually more interested in a child's overall well-being and happiness than they are in the subtler points of their child's mate's nature. And most parents are likely to keep most of their reservations to themselves.

But it's different with friends. To us, friends are an extended family, seeing us through good times and crises we'd never think to mention to our parents. Lovers may come and go, but friends remain constant. They turn up more often than just for an occasional Sunday dinner. We want to enjoy long, leisurely evenings with friends and lovers, to plan weekends or vacations together and we want our friendships enhanced—not stifled—by the presence of a new lover. So it is indeed nervous-making to be paraded before Sonny's best friend, Mark, whose wife was Sonny's ex-wife's college roommate, or Gladys's old friend Sam, who years ago was her lover until he came out of the closet and ever since has been the shoulder she leans on in the same way you talk to your analyst. Not only are these various characters interested in whether you and your lover are suited to each other, they also want to make sure you're fun to have around. Like it or not, you are already a subject for speculation among your lover's friends. They already know something about you, just as you've told your friends all about Raymond or

Margie. In fact, friends on both sides began to take part in your courtship long before this. They're there from the beginning.

An astute analyst of social trends in the last century observed that "The chief business of women is, first, to get married; second, to get others married." Customs change—now liberated men are just as free as women to meddle in other people's lives. So whether you're courting or not, it's always a good idea to watch your friends carefully to see what they have in mind for your happiness. Among some of them—particularly the newly in love, the newly living together or the newly married—your love life is likely to be a subject of great concern. If you're alert you'll probably sense a conspiracy among them to pair the world up neatly and in twos, what we might call a "Noah Complex." Since you're likely to be a target of this conspiracy if you're not dating—or a part of the conspiracy yourself if you are—it's worth giving a thought or two to when the rules of courtship should consider the unattached.

To begin with, the social world, with all its "couples," can be a daunting place during the times when you're on your own. Even with the divorce rate what it is and with people stocking up on Soup for One wherever you look, there are plenty who still believe, for example, that to have an odd number of guests at dinner is worse than serving Chinese take-out food right from the containers when everyone's in black tie. There are men and women who would rather spend an evening in their closets than be a third wheel at a party or in a restaurant. The unattached male, particularly if his socks match and he is generally presentable, is still in demand to "balance" this affair or that. What happens, unfortunately, is that the minute we get paired up again, we tend to forget the feelings of our unattached brethren, and how it felt only a few weeks ago, when we were in the same situation ourselves.

Many people who are single (myself included) find the invitation that requires them to "bring a guest" offensive, for example. It seems to suggest that on your own you're something short of an asset. There are times in every single person's life when, pure and simple, there is no guest to bring, when it would be easier to arrange for a trained sea lion than a date. Perhaps the person you're dating is busy, or you don't feel, for whatever reason, that you'd like to invite him or her. Perhaps you're not dating at all, and don't feel like dragging along a friend. Maybe you can think of things more objectionable than sitting at a dinner table next to a person of your own sex.

The bring-a-date rule thus may result in more trouble than it's worth: Many people, men and women both, will turn down invitations simply because they are too shy to insist on going alone. The dateless person should never be made to feel like a pariah. The suggestion that one bring a date if he or she would *like* to is, on the other hand, thoughtful and gracious.

Be grateful, then, to the host who is kind enough to inquire, "Will you be bringing a guest?" instead of asking the name of your mythical date. But be wary, too, because once you turn down the option of bringing the companion of your choice, you are vulnerable to the host who now sees the perfect opportunity to invite a guest on your behalf. You may be on your way to a blind date.

Actually, there are a couple of variations on the blind-date theme: first, when Cupid invites you over for an evening that will include as entertainment one or more unattached friends; and second, when Cupid tells his or her friends Hubert and Charisma about each other and leaves the rest up to them; whatever the case, often you are left to wonder, after the meeting, whether Cupid really is blind. Either way, both matchmaker and victim have a few responsibilities to keep in mind.

Cupid's primary duty is to be loyal to both friends, and to remember the principles of truth in advertising. To tell Hubert that "Charisma is my best friend *and* the most gorgeous creature you've ever seen" when Charisma is in fact much smarter and nicer than she is pretty, is doing a disservice to both sides. It's enough to play Cupid without trying to be someone's seeing-eye dog as well.

Furthermore, Charisma and Hubert are entitled to some say in the way their blind date is to be arranged. Some people prefer fix-ups that appear perfectly casual and spontaneous—just a few friends coming over for a good time, and if Charisma and Hubert happen to like each other, then fine. If Cupid wants to set things up this way, however, he or she should first check with Charisma and Hubert. This doesn't mean that Cupid has to say, "Will you come over for dinner and a blind date?"; state simply, and to both sides: "We're having a few people to dinner and I think Hubert—remember I told you about him?— will be able to come." The less pressure the better. It's usually wise to have a few additional guests, so that Cupid won't have to spend the entire evening scrutinizing Charisma and Hubert for the signs of instant love.

Many people I've talked to, though, would rather face the music one on one, away from their friends' watchful eyes—and here is where my friend Roger's Rules for Successful Blind Dating come in handy. Roger's theory is that a blind date is much like a job interview: Both parties have something to offer—whether they have something to offer each other remains to be seen. I'd trust these rules simply on the basis of Roger's (vast) experience; in addition, others have followed them with good results.

1. No matter how desperate you happen to be at the moment, never build up your hopes. Allow yourself no fantasies. Blind dates work on the same principles as direct-mail campaigns: a 2 percent return is a phenomenal success.

2. Never make a blind date for a weekend. For the working person, for someone juggling custody, for just about anybody, the weekend holds a psychological importance that Monday-through-Friday does not. A blind date for a Saturday, particularly if it turns out the way most blind dates do (see above), will disappoint you inordinately and will ruin what might otherwise have been a fine Saturday night with a good book.

3. Never make a blind date for dinner. You'll never know how interminable dinner can be until you're sharing it with the wrong blind date.

4. Never meet a blind date at your house. Your friend may not know your date very well, and your blind date may be casing your place for an eventual robbery. Start from scratch, on neutral ground.

5. A date for drinks makes for the best blind date. If you are dazzled, you can then arrange on the spot to be free for dinner.

6. Always report back at once to your Cupid, who is nervously awaiting your call. And think of at least one nice thing to say about your blind date.

Whether or not your friends have arranged the date that dazzles, they'll follow the progress of your romance from the beginning. Your head will be up in the clouds somewhere, but your friends will be in touch with you from Earth, reminding you to be careful, to try harder or less hard than you did last time, to remember that a bird in the hand is worth two in the bush or that a penny saved is a penny earned—all kinds of sensible advice that you will ignore because you are too busy falling in love to listen. Your friends will stand by you as you fall in love, no matter how you may bore them about it.

Friends understand by instinct, and because they too have fallen in love, that while you are off on your metaphorical honeymoon they won't see too much of you (although the good friend will take special care not to ignore his or her friends, as too many of us tend to do, while under the influence of a new love); friends expect, too, that, once you resurface, everything about the friendship will return to normal. And naturally these loving and trustworthy friends of yours will be *very* curious about your new lover who, after all, has been depriving them of your company during these past weeks or months; they may even be a little worried that your lover is spiriting you away. But by the time you're ready to "come out," they're ready, too; ready—like yesterday's parents—to judge whether this romance is in your best interests.

In rare cases it so happens that your lover already knows and perhaps shares many of your friends. Everyone may approve. You get to skip a step; your arrival together instead of separately won't much change the balance of the social circle. Some groups operate under the principle that "If you're good enough for Roy, you're good enough for me". But in many cases you or your lover may come to know how it feels to be a commoner presented at court. There are plenty of social circles where the first rule is: Never accept anyone new if you can possibly help it, or at least not until the neophyte has gone through a long initiation period. This outlook, of course, makes it more difficult to feel welcomed by your lover's friends.

In the old days, it was the custom to present new people first through a letter of introduction, which was great for the newcomer. The letter, which spelled out your credentials in flattering terms, would precede your arrival and force your new hosts to give you a fair chance. A nineteenth-century etiquette book described how this worked:

> Letters of Introduction are to be considered as certificates of respectability—as proofs that you are known by the introducer to be a proper person to be admitted into the friendly circle of him to whom you are recommended, without the risk, in these days of elegant exterior, of his harboring a swindler, or losing his spoons.

But now, when we meet a lover's friends for the first time, the introduction might have been made differently. Bristol may already have told his friend Haskins that, "Elizabeth is wonderful. Um, no, she's not separated yet, but she will be soon. Well, yeah, she's still seeing that other guy, too, but they're about to break up. Oh, I didn't mind buying her that fur coat; you should see how she shivers when it get cold. She hasn't moved in with me— she's only staying until she finds a new place, but she's got to find a job first. Yes, it's terrible that my art collection was stolen. No, no sign of a break-in." Some relationships are better in fact than on paper. In this case, even before they've met, Elizabeth has a lot to worry about where Haskins is concerned.

There can be complicated dynamics at work when friendship and romance come together. You and your lover will begin to see each other in a new, public way, once you see how your friends react to your lover and vice versa. Not all of your friends will like your chosen one; not all of his or her friends will like you. There may be hurt feelings to soothe; just because we're all grownups is no reason to assume that we're all going to act like grownups. Your loyalties might come into question: Which is more important, your best friend's fortieth birthday party or your lover's awards' ceremony? No wonder you might feel a bit jittery about bringing everyone together, at least at first. "Going public" is a momentous step.

Nearly everyone has a complaint about how he or she is treated vis-à-vis a lover's friends. "She drags me along to dinner with these friends of hers and all they do is talk about people I don't know"; "All his friends are older and married and all they care about are their children, houses, cars. What am I supposed to do—tell them about my cat?"; "She always wants to see *her* friends, but she never seems to have time for mine"; "He makes all these plans—we'll all have dinner on Saturday—and consults everyone else, but he doesn't bother to ask me"; "She's always in a good mood with her friends, but with mine she doesn't bother to try"; "His friends are boring"; "Her friends are boring."

I once read an article about a fifth-grade teacher who every year assigned her class "Little Red Riding Hood" to be re-written from the wolf's point of view—it's a very different story this way, and a good lesson to remember for anyone who's negotiating the sometimes difficult transition from "honeymoon" to reentry. You'll rarely go wrong if you try to imagine on each occasion how your lover feels, how your friends feel, how his or her friends feel and so on.

To begin with, it's a good idea to introduce new friends to old ones gradually, rather than all at once. To ask the shy Daisy to be co-host at your famous annual Christmas party—when she knows that your date last year was the gregarious Peony, whom everyone adored—isn't the ideal way to introduce Daisy to your friends, whether or not you think the gesture is a compliment. When too many of your friends are assembled at once your attention will be spread thin—and the odds are that Daisy, the stranger, won't get her fair share. Think ahead to whether your lover will feel comfortable before you begin to play social director. Start the introductions slowly: First pick a relatively normal friend or two and arrange an evening so that you can all get together.

It is always a mistake to try to tinker with either your lover's or your friends' personalities in time for the Event. People who say things like "You're not going to wear *that*, are you?," "Please don't tell that dumb story about the peanut-butter cups," "Could you just this once not burp at the table" or "I wish you'd get contact lenses" don't deserve good friends, much less lovers.

A little prepping, on the other hand, is entirely in order. You don't want to get into a situation where, trying to be friendly and make pleasant conversation with Susan's friend Margaret, you say, "I hear you're taking belly-dancing lessons," whereupon Margaret turns to Susan and says icily, "That was *supposed* to be a *secret*." The fact is, you already know more about Susan's friend Margaret than perhaps Margaret would like. You can be sure, too, that Margaret knows plenty about you. It's up to Susan to deflect any such breaches in intimacy before they occur. As any good host would, she will advise her guests ahead of time about what might make for good conversation and which topics should at all costs be avoided. Where your friends are concerned, your role is both host and intermediary.

You can't, for example, leave everything to fate, and assume that everyone will get along admirably while you sit back, detached, to watch—unless, of course, your lover and friends take to each other immediately. No matter how uncomfortable the role of host is for you, it's up to you to keep the conversation going (after all, these people are all here because of you) and to see that the occasion revolves around what interests all of you and not around people that your lover does not know, or the canoe trip you and your lover plan to take next month.

You will, of course, lapse into an occasional aside where one person will be left out in the conversational cold. But all you have to do when this happens is to say to the person who's left out, "Excuse us for two minutes while we dispense with this gossip," or to explain that "Mathilda is someone we knew in high school—now she's involved in a paternity suit." Such attentiveness, nothing more than common courtesy, makes all the difference.

These "rules" sound so simple, but according to many of the people I've talked to they're violated much more than anyone might suspect. A woman I know, for example, told me a chilling story about the time her "boyfriend" introduced her to a group of his ex-wife's friends; she was the first woman they'd met since the divorce. "They were unbelievably rude; I wanted to die," she said. "We were there for an entire evening and nobody ever spoke to me, not once. Even Paul (he was nervous about the whole thing too) ignored me. By the end of the evening, everyone was laughing together about old times and I was looking at the books in the bookshelves, crying. It was the most horrible evening in my life. I felt like the

Elephant Man." Paul apparently apologized later, but in cases like these apologies aren't enough; Paul was just as rude as his friends. His responsibility was to step in at the beginning on his lover's behalf; she was also, after all, his guest. An apology in such cases is nothing more than an afterthought.

A man I interviewed told me about a party to which he had escorted the woman he goes out with. "*Her* friends, I didn't know anybody." She disappeared the moment they walked in the door and was flitting from group to group as he, after making a few tentative gestures, stood on the sidelines. "Finally I went up to her when she was talking to some people," he said, "and she seemed kind of annoyed that I was there. We had a fight afterwards. I kept asking her why she had even invited me if she didn't want to be with me and she kept asking why I couldn't make friends. They just weren't very friendly people." Again, within reason, one's first responsibility is to one's date, particularly when your date is a stranger to your friends.

Teresa, a twenty-eight-year-old woman I talked to, still shudders at the memory of one particularly dismal evening. "He said it was a semi-business dinner and he'd really like me to go. I went as a favor. There were twelve of us at the table, all these men with their wives. They all played golf, they all belonged to the same club, they all knew each other. He was at the other end of the table from me, having a wonderful time; I was sitting there feeling invisible. So I did a really horrible thing: I pretended to go to the restroom and then I went home." I can hardly blame her; we've all felt the same temptation to get up and leave. Even so, she could have stayed and endured the evening. For his part, he could have helped by wandering down to her end of the table between courses to see how she was doing. Or he could have called across the table, "Teresa, what was the name of that actor the other night?" just to draw her out. What she really wished for was a little attention from her lover; if he had been even minimally supportive, she felt, she "could have put up with it."

Once you've seen that your date is at ease, the next thing to think about is your friends. The biggest complaint I've run into from this camp is how revoltingly affectionate people newly in love sometimes act around each other. The problem of inappropriate public display is nothing new—nearly twenty-five hundred years ago, Plutarch advised his fans, "How rude it is to kiss in the presence of third parties." An affectionate touch or an arm around a shoulder is fine, but much more than that will make the people around you uncomfortable.

Others complain about group-quibbling over checks ("I couldn't believe it! My friend looked at the check and told me how much I owed. He had divided it in two— he wanted me to pay for half his date."); lovers who dwell in a tiresome way on their love; or people who once they fall in love forget that you have to be a person, too, not just half a "couple;" or a friend in love who forgets what it's like *not* to be in love ("She came with us all the time when I was going out with Mark. But now she's going out and I'm not, and she never asks me along."). Like other emotions, love has to be adjusted to the occasion; there's no need to be silly about it, or to be careless about other people's feelings. There's no reason for friendship and love to be mutually exclusive.

Find yourself in any new social world and you'll soon hear about the tangles; you'll learn who has slept with whom, why this one left that one, how A and B managed to get together. Each social "tribe" has its own rules, rituals, ways of entertaining itself and criteria for membership. But what happens if, no matter how much in love you are, you don't feel at home in your lover's tribe? Or if he or she doesn't feel at home in yours?

In every grown-up relationship there are three separate lives intertwined—yours, your lover's and the life you share. What needs adjusting at this stage is the way these lives overlap, how much time each of you will spend in the other's world.

There's no reason to think, although some people do, that just because you've managed to corral a lover he or she is required to be at your beck and call every time you want to go out and play with your friends. Yet there is often a push-pull struggle when it comes time to fill in the social calendar. You want Dennis to come to the nightgown exhibit with you and your friend Glinda on the same afternoon he wants to check out the discarded auto parts at the junkyard with his friend Ralph. Or you want to spend Saturday night with your drinking buddy Boozer, while Anastasia wants to attend the housewarming party of some friends of hers who repainted their walls flamingo pink.

Most people end up living a balancing act, deciding from week to week who will attend what, and on which occasions you'll go together or separately. How the balance works out is different in each case, of course. You'll rarely end up in an "equal-time" situation, but you have to insist on your rights in order to come out with at least a fair settlement.

An American etiquette book published in 1860 pointed out that, "Here in New York, husbands and wives do not even go to the same parties unless they prefer to do so. It is presumed that they have enough of each other's society in private." A modern relationship can just as easily integrate separate lives and lives together, so long as the arrangements are fair and you're both willing to compromise when a command performance arises. Thus there's no need to tell Jeremy that the next time you see his friend David you hope it's at David's funeral—it's enough just to avoid David all you can. And remember *your* feelings about David the next time you insist that Jeremy accompany you and your friend Proclivity to her mother's recital for six flutes and a drum.

On the up side, there are many times when friendships and courtships come together in the happiest way, when your lover and certain of your friends strike up friendships of their own. Such extended arrangements work out even better when we attend to the finer points of etiquette. For example, a woman I interviewed was invited for Thanksgiving dinner to her boyfriend's married friends' house in the country. She was a little nervous about going. Her boyfriend kindly thought to ask his friends to call her up and assure her that she was included in the invitation. "The woman, whom I had met only once, was so nice. She told me what she'd be wearing and even let me bring a pie. I felt so much better about going." In return, she and her boyfriend entertained the married pair for a weekend in the city; in thanks, the couple sent each of them a plant. The plant of her own assured her even more that she was now a part of the friendship in her own right. Separate invitations for the courting couple, or separate thank-you notes (or even separate thank-yous) will make the newcomer feel much more a part of things.

I have a particularly pleasant memory of an evening I spent with a man I was once seeing and a close woman friend, whom the man I was with knew slightly. We had all three decided to go out for dinner, an occasion that seemed festive because it was a few days before Christmas. In an expansive gesture, which I really appreciated, my date paid the dinner check for the three of us, although on other occasions we might have split the check more equitably. Afterward we all decided to go somewhere else for a nightcap. On the way to the table my woman friend stopped for a moment to talk to the maitre d' who, a couple of minutes later, brought to the table a bottle of champagne she had secretly arranged to contribute to our celebration. Because I had brought together these friends who clearly were having a good time, I had rarely felt happier.

So it is that many things do work out well in the end — a good thing to remember when it comes time for a trauma even more terrifying than meeting a lover's friends: meeting his or her children.

The subject of children and lovers is big enough for a book in itself—but even a book couldn't possibly cover the infinite number of horrible things that can happen. Never is there a "test" in courtship more critical than winning the approval of some surly four year old who happens to belong to the one you love. You can always wangle your way out of difficulties with your lover's friends ("No, I think I'll skip dinner with you and Wally to-night"), but it's a different matter entirely to try to explain why you break out in hives every time you're in the same room with dear little Everett.

Before we go any further with this delicate subject, we might as well dispense with a few of the questions asked again and again, if only because misery loves company:

Q: Why is it that my lover lets his child behave badly toward me, when the kid couldn't get away with behaving that way toward anyone else?

A: Because he feels guilty.

Q: Why does my lover flinch when I so much as touch her arm in front of her children?

A: Because she feels guilty.

Q: Why does my lover make me sleep in a different bedroom when his kids come to visit, even though his kids and I get along?

A: Because he feels guilty.

Q: Why won't my lover ever stand up for me in front of her kids, even when she knows I'm right?

A: Because she's more afraid of her kids than she is of you.

Q: Are all kids this bad?

A: Not all, but a good many.

Q: What can I do to get my lover to see *my* side?

A: Not a whole lot.

Q: Why didn't I meet someone who doesn't have kids?

A: I don't know.

Q: Will the situation ever get better?

A: Maybe; maybe not.

When it comes to reconciling children and courtship, a parent is correct to anticipate a tough task ahead. Naturally you feel protective of your child, a little guilty about bringing someone else into the act, concerned that your lover and child get along well and worried that they won't. You find that you aren't as comfortable around your lover when your child is present, nor as comfortable with the child when your lover is around. On top of that, you read so much these days about how destructive divorce is for children, and you don't want your own child to suffer because of something you "did...."

From the child's point of view (and I speak as a child of divorce myself), families seem bizarre and confusing enough without letting strangers into them. You want your parents to get back together, no matter how unlikely this may be or how unhappy they were together, just because having a real family is probably better than not having one. You feel that your parent is pulling away from you, changing, acting a little differently now that he or she has fallen in love. Your own life is disrupted and you feel bereft. Instead of pancakes for breakfast, you're getting whole-wheat toast. On the other hand, consciously or unconsciously, you sense here a perfect opportunity to sabotage your parent in return....

Enter the lover, whose child this is not. When you fell in love, the child was a sort of background figure, out of sight, out of mind. But now the child is going to turn up in your life: Sometimes you find out about surprise parties ahead of time, yet when they happen they're somehow still a surprise. You are under pressure to see the unqualified beauty and brilliance of this child. You know that other people can question or criticize but you cannot. For your part, you feel that you're regressing—to the approximate age of the child in question. Most of all, you know that this child has the power to make you miserable, maybe even ruin your life.

Circumstances vary from child to child, parent to parent, age group to age group, and from one strategy of child terrorism to another, but after hearing dozens of tales related by hapless people whose lovers are also parents, one begins to wonder if perhaps the real victim of divorce is not the lover who unknowingly enters the picture later, like the gentle birdwatcher who, a year or two after a war has ended, innocently steps on a left-over mine that no one bothered to deactivate.

"Martha has these two little girls," a man I interviewed said, describing his particular victimization. "Every time I go over to pick her up they cry, they get sick, they miss their daddy, they're afraid to stay home. Half the time Martha tells the babysitter to go home and we end up staying with the kids. It's been going on for months. They're so spoiled. If she would stand up to them just once it would be the best thing for them."

From another man—this a man with kids of his own: "She lets this kid humiliate me. This sounds stupid, I know, but the other night I was playing 'Go Fish' with Jamie, her little boy, and he was cheating all over the place, looking ahead to the next cards. But I won the game. Then he started screaming that he had won the game and asked his mother who had won. 'You did, honey,' she told him. I just exploded. She made me look like a fool in front of this kid. Kids have to learn that they can't win every time. My kids don't behave that way, I wouldn't let them."

"Kids are so *mean*," says a woman whose boyfriend has two of the little darlings. "I called up his house once and this kid—she's thirteen—said, 'I think he's working things out with my mother. He doesn't want to talk to you.' My boyfriend just laughed when I told him. He thought it was cute." Another woman got a similar run-around over the phone: "He's not here. I thought he was with *you*." Several people complained about lovers who treat them like friends when the kids are around: "He acts so cold, as if I'm just somebody he hardly knows who happens to be there. His ex-wife has a boyfriend who stays over all the time, but when the kids come to visit him I have to pretend that I don't belong there. His kids don't respect me because in front of them *he* doesn't respect me." Or, "He always makes me go along with him and the kids to the zoo or the movies or whatever. But then he ignores me the whole time."

A friend of mine who is married and has stepchildren sums up the problem thus: "It's as if they don't think they can be good parents and in love at the same time. It's a one-or-the-other thing. A lot of kids know this and just walk all over the parents." In fact, kids are not only resilient but insightful about their parents' weaknesses and guilt, and how to take advantage of them. If there's a power struggle going on, in many cases it's not safe to assume that the grownup has the edge. So to even the odds, let's imagine Papa; his gentle girl friend, Nanette; and his adorable little Trixie.

MYTHS THAT PAPA (AND OTHER PARENTS)
SHOULD FORGET THIS VERY MINUTE:

1. Little Trixie wants her Papa to fall in love and be happy.

2. Children are said to be good judges of character. Maybe since Trixie doesn't like Nanette I should take another look myself.

3. Little Trixie needs to get all her feelings out in the open. Nanette will just have to understand if Trixie is unspeakably rude.

4. At least I don't have to worry about Nanette's feelings. She's a grownup and will understand.

5. They'll get along sooner or later, or at least get used to each other. So I should just step back and let it happen.

It's difficult sometimes to be clearheaded about an issue so dense with emotion, especially one where each faction has a set of rights—and where the rights are in absolute conflict.

Papa, for example, *does* have the right to be happy as a parent and happy in love. But little Trixie also has the right to her Papa's attention, devotion and love. And of course poor Nanette has the right to a proper boyfriend. Simple. But remember that little Trixie really doesn't want Nanette around at all—and Trixie wasn't Nanette's idea, either. Sooner or later, it's almost impossible for poor Papa to avoid hurting either Trixie's feelings or Nanette's; we are dealing with natural adversaries. If ever a situation requiring manners existed, this is it.

The first rule to remember is that a parent/lover can never legislate affection, so if you're a parent don't even try. You can't make your child like your lover; you can't make your lover like your child. Sometimes they'll like each other; sometimes they won't. However, you *can* legislate if not respect then at least the outward appearance of respect.

As is the case with friends, it's best to bring children and lovers together gradually. The first meeting, experts and all people with a grain or more of common sense agree, should be unthreatening and casual—and not over Sugar Pops at eight o'clock one surprising morning. You as the parent have to decide how much of a "friend" your friend should be at the beginning—but remember that kids are smart and you can't, nor should you want to, deceive them about your relationship forever.

What will your child be most afraid of once you have a serious "friend"? A million things, but some fears are easy to figure out and put to rest from the start. In *The Kids' Book of Divorce, By, For and About Kids*, a bunch of eleven to fourteen year olds asked one another, "Do you want to meet your mother's or father's date?" and answered: "You may not want to meet their date because you are embarrassed or afraid of them or afraid of what they're going to say about you or what they might do to you mentally or possibly, physically. They might shower you with gifts and try to win you over from your true parent. On the other hand, they might be really nice and not do this." These are heartbreaking fears, and obviously both parent and "friend" must do everything possible to anticipate, understand and assuage them.

From divorced parents I've picked up some tips on introducing lovers that sound sensible—and respectful of the child. "Don't spring a friend on them," a mother advises. "My kids don't like surprises and it's best to tell them ahead of time that someone's coming to visit." From a father: "I once told my daughter she was really going to like my new friend. After they met, she started sobbing. She said, 'You promised I would like her and I don't.' Now I say, 'I *hope* you'll like her.'"

"Mention the other parent in the child's presence, so it won't seem like you're asking him to switch loyalties," a father of two sons suggests. "But for God's sake tell your girl friend what you're doing." A mother has learned that it's better to, "Plan something fun to do. Don't just sit around and stare at each other." And for all concerned, "make the first visit short."

If after all your efforts the visit still doesn't seem to be working out, you may have to take the matter out of fate's hands and put it in your own. "If it's not working out, you can't pretend it is," says the mother of a six-year-old boy. "Stop everything, take the child aside and ask what's wrong, right there. I did that once and my son cheered right up—I think he just wanted me to notice that he didn't like the whole idea. Another time, I took him into his bedroom and he cried for a while. We stayed there together until he was better, then he was willing to go out and try again."

Most lovers understand that for the first few get-to-gethers their feelings will have to come second. At first, the most important thing is for the child to feel comfortable. "So you put up with being ignored, or walking in the weeds while they're taking up the sidewalk," says a friend of mine. "You feel so *alone* at first." A little later on, however, the parent should realize that children between the ages of about four and eighty-six must be made to understand that Mommy or Daddy has a life both as a grownup with grown-up friends and needs *and* a life as a parent, and that these are often separate. A child who is loved and cared for will receive the message that he or she is loved; granted, it may (even under the best circumstances) take thirty or forty years for the message to get through, but it *will* get through. Thus many parents must stop worrying that by caring for an "outsider" they are somehow violating the obligations of parenthood.

Once you've reassured your child, it's time to reassure your lover, who might not wait around thirty or forty years for the proof of your love. In many cases this involves standing up to a pint-sized guerrilla. One of the biggest grievances "step-friends" have is that children are permitted to be rude to them simply because the parent is afraid that discipline on their behalf will alienate the child. Nonsense. Parents don't allow their children to be so rude to other people, do they? Why, then, should a parent permit a child to be rude to someone he or she particularly cares about? It will not harm a child (and it might do a world of good—we all have to learn at an early age that we have to do things we don't especially feel like doing) to say to him, "Tommy, you're being very rude to Mommy's friend James. Apologize this very minute." It's not enough for Mommy to apologize to James. Even the children of divorce must learn the fundamental rules of being civil. (There may come a time, too, when James and Mommy will have to have a confrontation about Tommy. But sometimes the situation will improve on its own; it should be given that chance.)

The lover, too—or the Interloper, as a woman I know calls herself—will have an easier time of it by following a few simple rules. The first, as I learned from *The Kids' Book of Divorce* and from memory, is to avoid bearing gifts, at least at first. Kids know when someone is out to bribe them. It also won't help to brood or worry too much about whether little Adam will like you. Hope that he will—and hope, too, that he wants to like you as much as you want to like him. The most touching compliment you'll ever receive from your lover's child is to be considered his or her friend. That's trust. So don't try to be parental (kids have enough authority figures), austere, overly jolly or anything else you're not: Be yourself, and leave the rest to time and fate.

After you've been through Louis's friends and Louis's children, meeting a boss, parent or even an ex-spouse will seem like a piece of cake. You've come pretty far. As time goes on, as you and your lover grow more serious about each other, some of the problems that might have arisen with friends and relations will get worse—others will go away. The more real your love is the more likely it is that you can solve whatever problems do come up. Very likely your love does feel more "real" now: You've tried it out in the world; you've seen it in a number of different settings. Instead of your friends' asking, "What are you doing on Saturday?" they might more naturally ask what you and Saul are doing. You've broken the ice with the children, if that was something that had been worrying you, and perhaps you and the children get along fine. You might already have met each other's parents. The questions about your future that you've been unwilling to think about all this time are popping up more and more now, and you're thinking more about your relationship itself, perhaps talking with your lover about what will happen next. The world you inhabit and the world your friend inhabits don't seem so distinctly apart anymore; they overlap here and there. A generation or two ago you might have thought of yourself as "engaged to be engaged" or "engaged to be engaged to be engaged." We don't have a sentimental term for this stage these days, but something is going on. And all of a sudden your romance seems to be snowballing into something even more exhilarating than the first time you thought maybe you loved this person.

Chapter Ten

Relationship Blues

IMAGINE A scene in which a man and woman make Saturday night dinner reservations at a fashionable restaurant. They arrive, check their coats and are seated; they seem pleased with their table. The waiter brings a basket of bread, two glasses of water, a couple of menus and the wine list. A few minutes later he returns, recites the specialty of the day and waits expectantly to take their order. "No, no, we're fine, thank you," one of them says. "We really don't want to order any dinner."

Now imagine a situation where a man and woman meet at a party and plan a date for a few days later. They go out and have a wonderful time, then go out again and start a love affair. Soon they are an "item." A few months into this arrangmeent, one of them, perhaps in a romantic moment, brings up the subject of their future together. "No, I'm fine this way, thank you," the other one says. "I really don't want to get involved." Like the waiter, the person who has raised the subject of the future is likely to be puzzled at first, and then angry. Doesn't the waiter have the right to expect his customers to order dinner? Isn't that what a restaurant is all about? And doesn't a lover have the right to expect that courtship has something to do with the future? Why go into a restaurant if you don't want to eat—or into a relationship if you don't want to get involved, whatever that may mean?

Far-fetched as the analogy sounds, many restaurants do establish a minimum charge, just to keep the riffraff away. As for romances, there are many, many people—call them riffraff if you like—who see no connection at all between making hay while the sun shines today and making hay in a slight drizzle ten years up the road. To such people, the idea of commitment to a relationship is as appealing as commitment to a mental institution would be. You can recognize these people immediately. For one thing, they're everywhere. You've probably fallen in love with a few of them already, if you're not one yourself. Mention the word commitment in the presence of such a person and he or she will look around wildly and in fear. Like all disturbed people, these nervous lovers will scream and fight all the way to commitment.

In a 1906 book called *Eediotic Etiquette*, Gideon Wurdz (from what I could tell, a pretty eediotic guy himself), wrote that, "The Protective Tariff of American society is marriage.... It encourages the Domestic Enterprise and protects the Infant Industry." If anything, there's been a "tariff revolt" since those simpler days: The big taboo of our day, the big threat to the Studio Apartment Industry, is marriage. Except among the married, when the subject of marriage comes up today, most of us are likely to be reduced to embarrassed shyness, infantile giggles; we blush and look away. The unspoken agreement is that you can talk all you want about drugs, sex and rock 'n roll, so long as you don't mention heavy commitment or marriage, especially if you want nothing more than to get heavily committed or married yourself.

Along about this stage, several things are going on simultaneously in our courtship sequence. In some ways your romance will seem to be running by itself, to have settled into its own rituals. After a while you'll know, for example, that you automatically have plans for the coming weekend. Everything about your lover doesn't seem new to you, as it did so recently, now that you've grown used to each other. You don't worry about being seen in those socks with the holes in the toes. Your love affair needs fewer explanations now. You no longer have to say, "Remember that guy I told you about? No, not Bob. Bob was the one with the leaky waterbed. Bill—the one with the horseshoe collection. Right. Well, he and I...." You can simply say "Bill and I" and the people around you will know who and what you're talking about. You may find that you're no longer thinking only about what's happening in your own life. You're beginning to think for two: Will he like that record album you'd like to buy? Would she mind stopping to pick up your new guitar strings, since you're going to be late? What should the two of you buy Dora for her birthday? Couldn't you, by pooling your resources, afford a weekend away somewhere in the sun?

Partly what's happening is that the magic you've been feeling has mellowed into something more like ordinary affection. "In the beginning everything is so romantic," an old friend of mine once observed. "You want to be together all the time. But then after a while you go back to being yourself. You begin to realize that it's dumb and inefficient to take a shower together when you could be taking a perfectly fine, even better shower all by yourself. You don't feel like waiting around anymore when you want to use the soap."

But there's a magic to the ordinary, too, when you're in love. It might bring tears to your eyes when you see his model airplane kit spread out all over your dressing table, for example, or you might be profoundly touched every time you see that expression of determination she gets when she takes out her violin to practice. Familiarity enhances qualities about your lover you may not have noticed even a couple of months ago. You know that underneath it all he's really shy, but you can tell now when he's trying to pretend he isn't. Or you can sense that she's got something on her mind just by the way she rearranges herself into a certain position in bed.

Your relationship is sailing along, as if set on cruisamatic, according to the "rules" you set up for it some time back. Perhaps you take turns cooking dinner and cleaning up; staying over at one house or the other; paying for your dinners out or movies; deciding whose friends you'll see. You're used to sleeping together, and you're not surprised anymore when you wake up next to this person who used to seem so odd to you in the mornings, so out of place. The routine feels right.

It's along about this time, too, that one or the other of you will notice you've lost track of where the future is supposed to be relative to the present—or rather, that the future is something one is supposed to be thinking about and planning for all the time. For all your contentment, you look around and notice that the lives of the people around you seem to be forging ahead: this one has gotten married, that one's pregnant, so-and-so has a new job, someone you know has just bought a new house, your friends Al and Sal have moved into an apartment together. Just yesterday you were happy. Today—

now you can see it clearly—your life is going nowhere. So one or the other of you decides that it's time to Talk About the Future.

I'm always amazed by how two people can perceive the same world in such different ways. I remember going to see *Scenes from a Marriage* with the man I was seeing at the time—it's a painful movie to see with someone you care about—and I also remember being as affected by the dynamics between the two of us as I was by the movie itself. Depending on the scene, he would draw closer to me or pull away, as if I had just poked him with an electric prod. Afterward, I was certain that something momentous had happened between us at that movie, but apparently he didn't notice, for two weeks later he asked me, "Have you seen *Scenes from a Marriage* yet?"

A friend of mine called me at the office the other day, miserable because he and his girl friend had just had one of those early-morning fights that can leave you trembling and upset all the way to five o'clock. He had been in the wrong, he felt. Their plan was to meet that evening, presumably to continue the fight, and he decided to buy her a card and apologize. I called him the next day, checking in to see what had happened. He had shown up contrite, bearing as a peace offering a Hallmark "I'm sorry" card, but she by then had forgotten about the fight that had preoccupied him all day: "She didn't know what the card was for, even." Again, same world, different response to it.

Or you and a friend can read the same newspaper one morning and discuss what you've read; it will seem as if you've read different papers. "Did you see the article about the guy who turned his health club into a chicken farm?" "No, but did you read the front-page story about the psoriasis epidemic?" "No, I didn't see it." A woman

I interviewed had been going out for a while with a man she adored. She had been studying, as if for an exam, all the details of his life, learning everything she could about him. After six months of this, he wrote her a note about something—Dear Ann. Her name was Anne. She was crushed. And some married friends of mine, both thirty-five, have begun to discuss what many of us now refer to as the "baby thing." Both want a baby. "There's plenty of time," he says. But she says, "There's no time. We have to do it now."

If there's this much discrepancy in how we perceive the here and now, you can imagine, if you don't already know, what happens when two people start to talk about the future. The future could be an urgent matter to one of you, of not much immediate concern to the other. Locking up your relationship—deciding, that is, what's to become of the two of you—might seem like a simple yes or no decision to one of you, and as much of a riddle as the latest computer game to the other. But once you open up the subject of the Future, you'll see that you've raised not one but many questions.

You'll see first that very likely you won't be able to reach a clear agreement about what it is, exactly, that's going to happen in the Future. When you try to pin down an idea as elusive as happiness, you'll find that you're not as sure as you thought you were of what you have in mind. Even worse, you might not be able to agree on *when* this Future will "happen." Is the Future going to happen in six months? Will you get married in a year? Will you start living together after she finishes the last fourteen semesters of medical school? Or will the Future just happen on its own, someday?

Then there's the question of how real the Future should be in the present: "If we're going to get married and have a baby in two years then why *shouldn't* I talk about it now? What's wrong with telling a few people?" On top of all that, once the subject of the Future has been broached, the easy comfort of the present is never the same again. The Future becomes the reference point by which you judge the present and even the past, and everything you say and do takes on a different cast: If we're going to live together why did you buy a new stereo when I already have one? If we're going to have a baby what's that brochure, *Sterilization the Easy Way—While U Wait*, doing here on your dresser? If we're going to live happily ever after why did you tell Pete that you might go explore the Amazon for a year by yourself? If we're going to be together, don't you think you could have asked me before you signed up with the Marines?

Instead of the intensity you felt at the beginning, the excitement of newness and possibility, what you're experiencing now is the intensity of real life. There's more at stake in your relationship now; you've invested a lot of energy, time and love in it. Losing this person you care about would hurt you, maybe more than you let on. On the other hand, if you're really so much in love how come everything seems so confusing to you? Isn't love supposed to clarify things (like your life), not confuse them even more?

As it turns out, love is a many-faceted emotion. For most of us, the acts of loving and being loved are tied together with other expectations, other parts of our lives: It's almost never enough to leave love at that. We feel that when we're in love there has to be more. We feel that love will somehow change our place in the world, or perhaps that love will "solve" this problem or that.

Commitment means different things to different people, but in almost all cases we ask for "proof" of love—if you love me we'll get married; if you love me you'll leave me alone. Along with this need for proof we ask assurance, public and private assurance, that we're loved: You can say all you want to that you love me when we're in bed together, but it won't "count," it won't be real, unless the world knows we care about each other too. That's where the future comes in. In the world's eyes, love means certain conventional things—living together or getting married, children perhaps; an acknowledgment that two people in love are two people who are *together* in a fundamental, public way.

When one of you starts talking about commitment, the issue is really this kind of affirmation. The kind of affirmation, by the way, that has always been attached to courtship and love.

What's new to courtship now is not the expectation that love will lead to a whole chain of events, but rather the idea that to expect more from love, to expect promises or Futures or something to "happen" as a result, is bizarre and inappropriate. It's new to think that because someone wants to plan a life together with the person he or she loves, that someone is out of line, asking too much. In fact—and I hope you're sitting down for this one—the person who is curious or concerned about the future is in no way deranged. There's nothing abnormal about wanting to take one's life in hand, put one's affairs in order and get on with the future. There's also nothing wrong with looking at dishes, if dishes turn you on, or even at baby carriages, if it comes to that. These are perfectly normal acts and desires.

With due attention to the equal-time principle…it's also perfectly normal to want to procrastinate with such life-changing decisions, to have nightmares about being trapped in a china cupboard and not being able to get out. Sure, you want all of these things one day too, but there's no rush. You don't feel that you have to decide right this minute. Yes, yes, you love Imogene or Harry and can't really imagine that you won't be together always, but why do you have to make a commitment? What's wrong with things the way they are? I'm happy, you're happy, can't we just be *happy* for a while? Just because the Future is decided within two hours in the movies doesn't mean that's how it happens in real life.

What happens most often in our relationships is that we go back and forth, back and forth about the future for a long time, sometimes for years, or until somebody gets seasick and bails out. Even so, once the subject is out in the open, or at least partway out, everything you do will pull you a little closer to the Future, or else make it seem a little farther away. No matter which "side" of the debate you're on (and very often we take turns taking sides), it will be clear that something—the Future—has come between you. And from then on, even the simplest everyday transactions will reveal all kinds of things about what direction your love affair will take.

There's a subtle game I've observed men and women playing, either intentionally or unintentionally, once they've gone from romance to relationship. For want of a title, we'll call the game "Pronouns"—the Russian Roulette of love. To play Pronouns, all you have to do is adjust the structure of your dialogue to be sure to include, or exclude, your opponent, your lover. To do this, you can say "I" when you could as easily have said "we," or you can say "us" when it would be more accurate to have said "me." You can also choose carefully before you say either "mine" or "ours." The game is complicated, and it's usually played by people whose future together is uncertain—all the more reason that it can be so telling.

Only a few years ago, falling in love was like getting a piece of chewing gum stuck on your shoe. Once the gum or the lover was lodged firmly in place, it was impossible to get rid of. As gum will, your lover became a permanent part of your life, your consciousness. You found yourself part of a couple. You said things like, "We're Democrats," or, "We like to barbecue in the summer."

Now we're freer. We're allowed, even expected, to keep an "I" identity intact throughout a love affair and beyond. Still, there's a "we" dynamic implicit in love, a point at which, at least to a certain extent, "I" turns into "we." For the man and woman contemplating a future together, every "I" (I'm going to do this or buy this; my car, my house, my life, my plans for the weekend) can make your lover feel like a bit player in the overall picture of your life. Conversely, every "we" (we'll go here, we'll have such-and-such kind of a future; our house, our car, our life) can make you feel as if you're losing track of *you*, giving up your identity to couplehood.

A friend of mine lives with a man who was separated when she met him; now he's close to his divorce. Divorced herself, she's more than willing to understand that it takes time to recover fully from a breakup, but she feels that her companion is going too far. "He talks about his marriage as if it's in the present tense," she says. (She's an English major, and very careful about these things.) "He'll say 'my wife' or 'we have this green carpet upstairs.' It's *her* carpet now. And she's his ex-wife." When he isn't being loyal to his former "we" status, he switches into "I" gear. "If we're out with other people he'll say, 'I live in this tiny apartment.' It's embarrassing. I live there, too." My friend felt that "we" reminded him of his earlier life and marriage, that he wasn't yet ready for a new "we" and that "I" was the only identity he had left. And she knew that they couldn't build a proper life together until he acknowledged that he and she were a legitimate "we" in their own right.

Another woman I met is sensitive to the same issue. "Steven and I were having dinner with some friends the other night, and someone mentioned a new restaurant, one that we'd gone to a couple of nights before. He said, 'I went there on Tuesday.' I just sat there, didn't say anything. I should have said, 'You were there on Tuesday!? What a coincidence, so was I.'"

Or the pronoun game can be played the other way around. Still another woman complained about a man she had known who "used to come over to my house and say, 'We don't have any coffee,' or 'What are we going to do about this?' or whatever. He made me feel so closed in. I don't want to be that kind of a couple." To retaliate, this woman would purposefully phrase her statements so as to exclude him: "Instead of saying 'let's go to the store,' I'd start saying things like, 'The store has to be gone to.' The whole thing just got too ridiculous."

Other people notice how their pronouns change, depending on how they happen to be feeling at any given time. "I know when I'm doing this," says one man who recently began living with a woman he's been seeing for about a year, "but sometimes I'll say 'our' apartment, and other times I'll say 'my' apartment. 'Our' sounds so legal or something. It makes me nervous."

Interpreting Pronouns psychologically isn't very difficult: this one's afraid to be involved; that one's afraid to be alone. Most of us swing both ways, at one time or another. On my questionnaires, I asked, "When does 'I' turn into 'we'?" The most thoughtful answers were those that placed accuracy and courtesy above emotional intent.

For instance, suppose Clarette and Spenser go to the movies on Monday night, to see *The Drano Story*. It's a dreadful movie and they leave halfway through it. On Thursday they visit their friends Fred and Lucy, who ask them if they've seen any good movies lately. Spenser answers, "I saw *The Drano Story* the other night. It was awful. I left." Spenser is playing Pronouns. He's excluding Clarette not only from the conversation with Fred and Lucy, but also from the movie on Monday—and in effect excluding her from her own life. What's Clarette supposed to do throughout the rest of the conversation, smile vacantly? Spenser has not only been inaccurate in telling his story but insulting to Clarette as well. How much nicer to say, "Clarette and I saw *The Drano Story* the other night. We left in the middle. I thought it was awful, didn't you, Clarette?"

Even if you're timid about allying yourself with someone else, there's no reason to be unkind about Pronouns, or to worry that by uttering an occasional "we" you'll sound like an article on togetherness from *McCall's* magazine. Use "we" when it's more accurate to do so, and no one will feel left out. Use "I" for accuracy in the same way. That's the only rule you need to know. Important as it is not to lose sight of your own self, it's also human and comforting to be part of a "we" sometimes, so long as you don't forget the you that preceded the we. It's a sign of weakness, not of strength, to be without the capacity to share at least some of your life with another person.

While we're on the subject of sharing, we ought to talk about how to dole out the responsibility for financing the romance. No small task, this, and I've put it off this long simply because I don't like talking about money any more than you do, especially when it's mixed with love. An etiquette book published in the 1940s covered the subject in a single sentence, advising the woman that before marriage she was never to pet, never to pay. Forty-some years later, I can testify that it costs more to be in love than it does to be unattached. And oddly enough, many people of both sexes feel the same way: "I spend money like crazy when I'm going out. I can't afford to be in love."

I once sat on a train in the seat behind a young man and woman, both in their mid-twenties. Eavesdropping, I noticed that the guy was busily calculating figures while the woman was reading her paperback. After a while the man looked up and said, "I figured out the whole weekend. You owe me thirty-four dollars." Without missing a beat or looking up from her book, the woman replied, "You're crazy. I paid for everything."

Sometimes you can get along in a romance for months without ever discussing the subject of money. This practice is dangerous, however, because after a while you'll each wonder if the other thinks you're cheap. And if one of you really *is* cheap, the other is bound to catch on right away. Most of us are more understanding about things like adultery than we are about basic cheapness.

It's easiest if you're both young and liberated, or old and liberated, and making the same salary, give or take. Fifty/fifty, worked out either by, "I'll pay this time, you pay the next" ("That way," a young woman assured me, "you definitely know there will be a next time."), or by check-splitting at the scene. In many cases, though, the man makes more money than the woman, but both rightly feel that the financial burden should be shared. (It's also possible that the woman makes more money. All things are possible.)

Karen, a woman I interviewed, once went out with a man who made a lot more money than she did, yet she liked to assume her share of the cost of courtship—and he was even more committed to that principle than she was. "He assumed I'd pay for half of everything," she said. Date after date, he'd suggest a restaurant more expensive than she could afford. At first she'd pay up, ignoring incidental realities like the fact that she was bouncing checks left and right. Finally, out of necessity, she began an "I can't afford it" litany and started to suggest less and less expensive things to do, which weren't much to his liking. Then she began to get annoyed. Usually he picked her up at home, she calculated, and she often bought wine and hors d'oeuvres for them to share before they went out. She had made dinner for him a number of times, and frequently served lavish weekend breakfasts. She concluded that the romance was actually costing her more money than it cost him, and she was far less able to afford it.

The next time they went out to dinner (the *last* time they went out to dinner, in fact), she brought with her an itemization of the dinners, bottles of wine and so forth she had paid for, and when he asked her for money for her share of the meal, she presented him instead with her list, divided it in two before his eyes and asked him for the money he owed her.

In all fairness, from the stories I've heard it appears that cheap women can be even cheaper than cheap men. Penny, a member of the Pincher family, stayed at my friend Bill's house once while he went away on business for a few days; she was to take care of his dog. "I couldn't believe it," he told me later, "she practically cleaned me out. Everything was gone when I got home: food, juice, toothpaste, toilet paper. There was an empty ketchup bottle on top of the (unemptied) wastebasket."

Apart from this fundamental kind of cheapness, an unfortunate character disorder which really shouldn't be allowed in polite company, the issue of money is not simply a matter of dollars and cents. You can't put a price tag, for example, on the energy with which one person may try to make up for the money he or she can't contribute to a romance. What if the poorer half of a love affair is always the one to bring flowers or the wine, to make the dessert, pick up the tickets, do all the legwork? Is that enough of a contribution? Or are you, in your calculations, remembering to take into account all the petty cash that goes into love? The toothpaste, the tennis balls, the orange juice, the midnight cab rides from one house to another, birth-control paraphernalia, the tux he had to rent for your friend's wedding or the dress you had to buy for his business dinner? Or what about that time she showed up at your house with a sweater she had knitted for you, but "didn't have any money" to chip in for the movies? Does yarn figure into your balance sheet? And doesn't he borrow money from you all the time, for gas especially, and forget to pay you back? Because of this flagrant borrowing, aren't you paying for at least your share?

Before the cost of your courtship begins to mount up like the national debt, it's time to face up to the issue of money. But don't call in an accountant yet; you don't need one, you're in love. Love, remember, is more important than money.

The first thing to do is to forget the idea that it's bad manners to talk about money. In this case it's bad manners *not* to talk about money. And the second thing is to erase from your mind the notion that a romance can be split fifty/fifty. It can't.

When temperate people go into a casino they go in with the idea in mind that, "I have this much money to play with and no more. I can have all the fun I want to with this money; that's what I'm here for." Wise lovers will go into a romance the same way, with "this much" money to spend.

Don't be ashamed if you're poorer than your friend; you can make up for lack of money with real generosity.

It's a good idea to establish from the beginning what your financial circumstances are, by saying things like, "I'd love to go. I could chip in about twenty dollars for that, okay?" When you and your friend are discussing what you'll do over a weekend, for example, offer suggestions based on what you can afford, not on what your friend can afford: "Why don't we go to that new pub? It's supposed to be pretty good and not too expensive." If your friend chooses to upgrade the plans, there's no need to split hairs over the cost; you're entitled to pay what you would have paid for the pub. Make sure you're contributing all you can—looking up movie schedules, treating to a meal or making a meal occasionally, buying tickets or surprises—every chance you get. If you're doing what you can to help from the beginning, you have nothing to worry about.

If, on the other hand, you're the richer of the two—and you find yourself getting poorer by the day—you might have to take a few steps in your own behalf. Before you do anything drastic (suing, for example), however, ask yourself whether your friend possibly is spending money on your relationship that's not immediately apparent. No? Okay, it's time to say, "I can't afford this. Could you pay half?" You have to bring to your friend's attention the fact that you're not made of money, even if you are, along with the fact that you don't like being used. And you *are* being used if, in this day and age, you can't believe that you're paying for the whole thing. After a few "I-can't-afford-this" nights out most people will catch on.

Disagreements over money, unpleasant as they can be, are most often not a matter of who pays for what; who pays for what can usually be settled by a few subtle or not so subtle hints, or a couple of years with a shrink.

More quarrels arise, I think, over entanglements that mix money with emotion. How could Hector, who's supposed to be saving up so that you and he can rent a house for the summer, have blown his entire paycheck on a home computer he doesn't even know how to use? If Eloise is too broke to chip in for season tickets to the opera, how come she's bought all those new clothes? No wonder you and Morris can't go away—he spends way too much money on his kids.

We start out in a relationship with "my" money and "your" money. As the two lives draw closer together, as expenses begin to merge, a portion of the money tacitly becomes "our" money—money that's spent enhancing the relationship, or preparing for the future. Money keeps things going, and if one party feels that the other's not pulling his or her weight financially, he or she may also feel that the other doesn't care enough. Thus the woman who offers, on a rainy Saturday morning, to go to the store for bacon and eggs—then turns around and asks you for grocery money—might not be trying to rip you off; instead, she may be "testing" to see whether you like the idea of your lives being joined in a financial way. Similarly, when one or the other of you says from time to time, "Let me pay for that," it might be another way of testing out the idea of "our" money.

Before jumping to financial conclusions about your lover, then, it's a good idea to ask yourself whether there's an issue at stake that is deeper than who's going to shell out the next ten bucks. Men and women have always joined their fortunes as a result of a successful courtship; marriage, after all, was an economic institution long before it was a matter of love. Hence money problems in relationships today are often traceable to more abstract questions about the relationship itself. If you're sincere about your love in other ways, you'll rarely be called upon to spend money to "prove" it. Even so, money does play at least a symbolic part in every courtship. And you'll see that clearly enough the first time an occasion calls for giving a gift to your lover....

At first you think, "Oh, Christmas. How wonderful. I get to buy Reginald a present." The impulse is generous; it's a pleasure to buy a gift for someone you love. On second thought, however, you realize that a gift is worth a thousand words: Your gift will give away your true feelings. Suddenly it occurs to you that you don't know what your true feelings are supposed to *be*, how much love is the right amount to reveal. You see now the thrust of the problem: You want your true feelings to reflect, more or less, your lover's true feelings. You don't want to be caught in love red-handed with your gift of monogrammed silver if your lover is going to send you a poinsettia or a fruitcake. Technically, it's not what the gift costs that counts; it's what the gift *says*. But sadly, in our world, you can't say too much with a gift from the GIFTS FOR UNDER FIVE DOLLARS table.

A century ago, gift-giving was not a problem in courtship. Gifts were governed by the book. A lady could not "with propriety accept gifts from a gentleman *previously* to his having made proposals of marriage." (Once they were engaged, however, he could—and was expected to—bring her trinkets or "some trifling article of jewelry" all the time.) Fifty years later, the lady could welcome books, flowers and other impersonal items at any time. Interestingly enough, gentlemen were the ones who got shafted—they never got presents, it seems, until after the lady was safely married.

Today, if an occasion dictating a gift comes up early

in a relationship (say pre-honeymoon) it's easy to figure out what to do. By all means give a gift if you feel like it, and don't worry about getting something in return. You're in the whimsy stage. Something small is appropriate, something thoughtful enough to make a statement—but impersonal enough to make your statement ambiguous. A tape or a record, a couple of tickets to something your friend would like (not a wrestling match, if your friend is a woman who has never expressed a particular interest in wrestling), a memento of something you did together, a carefully chosen book—in short, your gift should reflect hope and mild affection.

It's also easy if you already have a couple of Christmases, birthdays or Valentine's Days under your belt. To allow for inflation and your deepening love, give something commensurately more profound than what you gave last year.

The in-between times—after exchanging "I love you"s and before deciding the Future—are sticky. What you don't want your present to do is to make your lover think, "I had no idea you felt this way." A gift too small or too big, something too impersonal or too personal, could, you feel, forever jinx your romance. Before we get to specific approaches, a few basic rules:

1. Never say it with flowers. Flowers are for apologies, or for "no reason except that I love you." Flowers are not legitimate presents for legitimate occasions.

2. Once you've said "I love you," never give a joke present, unless it accompanies a real present. The recipient doesn't take himself or herself as a joke, and you shouldn't either.

3. Never give a lethal weapon as a gift. A lethal weapon is a hostile gesture.

4. Don't give money or gift certificates to a lover. Money and gift certificates are appropriate only after you've been married for at least forty-five years.

5. Never give a gift that you could conceivably want back. By definition, a gift is not a loan.

6. If you're a woman, don't give a man boxer shorts with hearts on them. These were popular and racy gifts a few years back, and most men already have a drawer full of them, unused.

7. If you're a man and think there's the remotest chance that your lover might be expecting a ring, never give a gift in a box that could be a ring box. Your lover will inevitably be disappointed. Put your bracelet in a hatbox.

8. If your lover thinks that he or she will soon be getting married (to you), never give a gift that duplicates an item you already have, when two such items would be redundant for a marriage. Your gift will be construed as a good-bye present. No marriage, for example, requires his and hers sets of the *Encyclopedia Britannica*.

10. Whatever the gift, give it in private. You're lovers, and you're entitled to exchange presents alone, without family and friends watching to see how much in love you are.

What you really want to know, of course, is what your lover is giving *you*, or would be giving you if he or she were in your shoes. This, by the way, is not a crass thing to wonder about: You're not trying to save money—you're only trying to choose an appropriate symbol. So if you can, find out what you're getting or would be getting, if it were your birthday. If she's been leading you past a certain store window, asking you whether you like a certain polyester smoking jacket, you can put two and two together from that. Or if he has a close friend you can trust, ask the friend for advice.

Failing these tactics, start from scratch. Don't think first about money; think first about your lover. Study him or her from head to toe; spend a day in your mind with him or her. Notice what gives your friend pleasure. Hang out in his or her favorite stores. Forget about yourself and what your lover might *think*. Think instead about what will be fun, useful or a gift that will give your lover a measure of happiness. If you're worried about spending too much or too little money, choose a gift where the cost isn't the point. Go to antique shops or museum stores or anyplace that doesn't reek of consumerism. The *last* thing you should think about is money.

When you've decided on the perfect gift (an item your lover doesn't already have, one that won't embarrass either of you, one that's not more appropriate for your last lover than for this one), then think about its cost. Is it perhaps a little too expensive? Examine your feelings. If you can swing it and it's what you really *want* to give, then do it. If a gift by revealing your feelings makes you a little vulnerable, if it shows that you really do care, isn't that the point?

When you receive a gift in return, it's not fair to expect that because you've chosen to give from the up side of your feelings your lover will have taken the same risk. He or she has gone through the same process you have, and has experienced the same fears of being "caught" with the wrong feelings; perhaps cowardice or shyness won out in the end. If you expressed your feelings with your gift and your friend didn't express the same feelings, nobody is at fault. A discrepancy in gifts could reflect a discrepancy in feelings, or only a discrepancy in *expressing* feelings. There's a difference.

As for returning gifts to the point of purchase (as they say), all the etiquette books say you can. I myself have never had the heart to, unless it's clear from holding the thing up that your lover has you confused by at least four sizes.

It would be cheating to list actual gift suggestions here; the gift should come from you, not from a book. Besides, then *I* couldn't use all the ideas I've picked up from people gracious enough to tell me theirs.

All women love jewelry.

I'm always struck by how many love affairs can be conducted simultaneously between two people. There's you and your lover's idea of who you are. There's your lover, and your idea of who your lover is. There are the people each of you would *like* your lover to be. On the periphery are fantasy lovers, the lover you always dreamed about and the one your lover has imagined. Then there are the people you each hope to be one day, possibly the people you once were. There's the person you were on Wednesday—happy and confident, and pleased about the promotion just awarded you—and there's the person you are today, depressed and insecure, doubtful all of a sudden that this person next to you in bed really loves you as much as he or she says.

Just as it takes a few minutes at the beginning of a play to sort out which character is which, it takes time in a love affair to become acquainted with all these identities, and to see whether they'll get along. And even once you've made the acquaintance of some of them, it's still difficult to keep them all straight, let alone happy. In the pre-future stage of a relationship, getting all these "characters" to work together toward a happy ending (which happy ending?) is like trying to organize a kindergarten class at naptime.

First of all you argue.

It's useless to review the rules for productive arguing— we've all heard them and never paid a bit of attention.

(Never say never, as in, "You never…"; never say always, as in, "You always…"; avoid fighting at bedtime, during meals or before work; don't nurse disagreements; and so on.) And as much as we've heard these rules, we go on arguing in the way we always have: badly. If we could really learn to control or moderate our tempers, I suspect we'd all have made the effort by now.

It can be productive, on the other hand, to scrutinize your arguments to see if there's a common denominator to them. In most cases there will be: The fights in most relationships add up to about one fight. One fight, with infinite ways of showing itself.

Let's take Leah and Joey. On Monday they fight about Joey's unwillingness to go to Leah's parents' house for dinner on Tuesday. On Tuesday they argue because Leah has made a date for Wednesday with her old boyfriend, of whom Joey is jealous. On Wednesday, they fight because Joey refuses to sleep over at Leah's house, saying that it's eleven-thirty and raining and he's too tired to make the two-block trip. Thursday both have to work late and they have a fight over that. On Friday each of them is wearing a new sweater and they argue because they can't seem to decide if they should live together. On Saturday they attend a friend's wedding, and quarrel because Joey's kid hung up the phone on Leah. On Sunday they make love all day, talk about living together and don't fight.

Underlying all this tension is the fact that Joey and Leah are on the brink of deciding their future. All their separate identities are at war, battling because Joey and Leah are who they are—and also because they're not who they're not. Each identity is willful enough to want its say in what's going to happen, and each realizes that some of the "givens" will change once the ending of this story is settled. What we fail to think about in our relationships is the toll it takes on us to invest so much of ourselves, so much love, in a romance that could end at the drop of a hat.

Arguments have their own convoluted logic, and, for what it's worth, once we're in the no-man's-land between love and the resolution of love, most of our fights—using this logic—revolve around the unsolved issue of the future. Evenings not spent together, in fight jargon, are evenings that *would* be spent together if the future were certain. Money spent on sweaters is money not spent on planning for the future. Arguments, or so you think, over social commitments wouldn't turn into arguments if your lives didn't have to be planned piecemeal. Leah wouldn't mind so much about Joey's kid hanging up on her if she had a child of her own. Joey thinks he wouldn't feel jealous of Leah's old boyfriend if he knew Leah would come home to him after dinner. It's all the same fight.

You'd still fight, of course, maybe even have the same fights under different circumstances, if your lives were settled, if only because lives are never really settled and fights can never be avoided, except among zombies. But when love takes over a portion of one's life, as it does when a relationship begins to grow serious, the fear—after all this—of being hurt or being alone is bound to put pressure on your love, no matter how strong that love might be.

Beyond arguing out the future, you're still learning new things about your lover and your love. For all the plans and arguments, you can see that you're not really ready to say yes to anything important right now, much as saying yes is on your mind. Nor, if asked, could you bring yourself to say no to anything important. You're afraid, perhaps, that you could, even at this point, fall out of love, or that you might not yet be "enough" in love.

One question that many of us ask ourselves here is whether love should be "permitted" to disappoint us. "I mean, maybe I shouldn't have felt so affected by it. I'm twenty-eight," a man I interviewed told me, "but when my parents said they were getting a divorce I felt really bad. Really alone. So I called Paula and asked her to come over. But she had a job interview the next day and she had to wash her hair and read some stuff and wouldn't come." Of course love disappoints. Love is a bond between two fallible people.

Curiously, we're also, many of us, afraid to ask of love the very things we expect from it. I asked the same man whether he had told Paula how lonely, how needy, he had felt that night, and he said no, he hadn't. "I just thought she'd know."

We don't always know, we can't possibly. Falling in love is one thing; getting your bearings once you're there is another. Through trial and painful error we have to learn what hurts, so that we can avoid hurting. We have to learn how to help. We learn that lovers don't change themselves to fit our fantasies, and fantasies are such that we can't change them to fit those we love. Still, we muddle through somehow, trying to do the right things, the kind things. People who are capable of loving are always those most at risk. It's terrifying to give first your body, then your heart, to fall deeper and deeper in love and still not to *know* anything.

The time between now and the future can seem interminable to a lover, and there are ways for you to ease the tension of waiting and at the same time practice being in love; loving well is a habit that's acquired.

What many of us forget or don't recognize is that love requires sacrifice. There's not a whole lot of logic to that—love is supposed to make your life better, not worse—but it's true. You have to spend time doing things you don't want to do when you're in love; you have to give up your pleasures for someone else's; your territory is not exclusively your territory, nor your priorities your priorities, anymore. On paper, it doesn't sound so great. But love can be a matter of two wills bending rather than colliding.

If you really want to leave all possibilities for the future open, you'll have to make some changes in the present. Typically, one of the first such gestures is to give up a drawer to a lover, who then has a drawer, a stake, in your life. (Not that you can do much with a drawer, but it's a heartening symbolic gesture.) This shouldn't be a half-hearted "you can put some stuff in the corner of this drawer—don't mind the mothballs" gesture but a real gesture, a sacrifice on your part (you'll be scrunching up your own clothes). Practicing love.

Some people also exchange house keys or car keys, or you might end up with his and hers blowdriers at his and her houses. The point is that to feel truly a part of each other's lives, you'll have to make room in your territory, not just room in your bed.

At the end of the last century an etiquette writer complained that "the term 'courtship' as usually in practice defined does by no means necessarily include a desire of serving the noblest ends of matrimony," and then went on to ask: "In these interviews of the sexes, is anyone expected to appear in true garb or character?"

Okay, you can't predict until it's absolutely time to decide whether you're ready for the "noblest ends of matrimony." What you can do, what we all must do in love, is to display your "true garb or character"—especially once you've taken possession of someone else's heart. Fair is fair. Now you're all set...until the day when you find

the real-estate section of the newspaper laid out conspic-
uously under your morning coffee, opened to the section
advertising houses and apartments big enough for two.

Chapter Eleven

The Negotiating Table

On a hot summer day some time back I had lunch with a group of friends, among them a man and woman who had been married for about ten years. The conversation drifted lazily back and forth across the table, only partly shaded by a droopy umbrella; no one had much to say. As we were finishing up the last of the wine, someone wondered if perhaps it were snowing in the Himalayas. The married man seized upon this comment, sat up straighter and said that he had always wanted to be a mountain climber. His wife looked at him incredulously, then said to no one in particular, "Ten years. We've been married ten years. He's never once said anything about mountain climbing."

You can live a lifetime without knowing everything you'd like to know about your lover or your lover's feelings. Even your own feelings, much as you may think you know them yourself, will now and again surprise you: "You mean I said that? Are you sure? That doesn't sound like me."

Love affairs start when viscerally you sense certain qualities about someone who interests you, and when you also sense that there are even more things about this person that you *don't* know. The explorer's instinct takes over. With what little you do know, you set off to find out what you can about the rest. Throughout a courtship you're absorbed by all there is to learn; you're enchanted, surprised, changed by each new secret, each revelation.

After a while the secrets are fewer and farther between. You've heard all the really good stories; you know the punch lines to the jokes. You're not learning so much anymore, or so fast. You know what you know about Linda or Peter but, like the woman married to the would-be mountain climber, you see now that there are only so many things that are knowable. These are the borders of love. Beyond are all the things you don't—can't possibly—know. Twenty, thirty, forty years of loving and you'll still never be certain whether your love will last, or whether your lover will suddenly turn into someone you never expected. When the enormity of all these things you'll never know sinks in, the awful risk, the catch-22 of loving finally becomes clear. Those of us who spurn love or are afraid to take the risk are in fact more frightened of what we don't know, the mysteries that can't be solved, than of what we do know.

Still, a time comes in almost every relationship when you've gone about as far as you can go. Your love can't grow any more with "things" as they are now. You're in love, but you're stalled. You're moving neither forward nor backward. For all its pleasures, your love is immobilizing you, holding back the rest of your life: You see no point in buying new sheets at a white sale because aren't you supposed to get an apartment together—and presumably a queen-sized bed—as soon as you can find a place you can afford? You find it irritating to be paying two separate rents every month when you spend all your time in one house or the other. Your kitchen needs repainting but why do it now, with your life so unsettled? Your friends are beginning to speculate on when you'll be getting married; your parents long for grandchildren. You can't figure out where anything is anymore, with half your stuff in one place and half of it clear across town. The drawer you have at your lover's place, which at first made you feel so special, now seems simply inadequate: You're living a good part of your life out of that one drawer and you feel crowded. Moreover, there's a tension in waiting for the next step—the big step—in love, as if you've just gone through four arduous years of college only to find that you aren't going to graduate after all because you're one phys-ed credit short.

The exuberance of falling in love is over. You've already fallen. You're still in love, yes, but the feeling now is dominated not by fantasies of how love will turn out but by what it actually is here and now, by the mundane concerns of living in love: Don't forget that we have to go to Fred's on Saturday; It's your turn to go out in the rain for the bagels; Let's just stay home tonight—I'm tired; Have you seen my frisbee? To keep the momentum of your love alive, to keep your feelings and your lives moving in new directions, you'll have to take the next step. It's time to cook, as it were, or get out of the kitchen.

I wanted this book to have a happy ending. I thought it would be great to be able to say that by passing through all the stages of courtship and by doing X, Y and Z, you'd have a pretty good chance of emerging intact and with the ending you want. A hundred years ago, that's more or less the way it worked: very few people then had the fortitude to endure the disapproval they'd face by sneaking out of a romance so close to the end, by failing to live up to their obligations. But everyone else made it to the church on time.

Not today. There are plenty of happy endings, of course, but we've all seen surprise endings too, when one person or the other backs out of a romance just before signing the lease, or just after making all sorts of big promises. We've all seen someone hurt. Most of us have ourselves been hurt; as the song goes, "Love's been a little bit hard on me." As we see it, marriage is not the obligatory finale to courtship. Court all you want—marriage is something else again. The person who leaves a relationship unceremoniously at the last minute doesn't face the humiliation he or she would have found a century ago, either. There might be curiosity ("I don't get it. They seemed so happy"), or criticism of the *method* ("She shouldn't have walked out like that two days before Christmas"). But it's no longer within our sense of propriety to think, "He should have stayed with her. He did something dishonorable in leaving, after all that." Love and responsibility are separate virtues today, not bound together as they used to be.

This new "ethic" gives us a lot of freedom. We can experiment with love all we want. We can fall in and out of love dozens of times with no sense of duty attached to the act of loving. We're free throughout a love affair to think first of ourselves. You're leaving now? It's getting too heavy? But I thought. Never mind. Hey, no problem, see ya.

There's a lot about this "ethic" that's simply not right. We're not talking about chaste little flings where even at the end nobody has much to lose, or about affairs where the end was always in sight, even at the beginning. Although we may deny it, most of us do enter into love with expectations, even conventional expectations. Unlike our ancestors who were never so unwise as to give *all* of themselves from the first, when we fall in love we hold very little back. We truthfully confide things "I've never told anybody before." We grow accustomed to sharing a bed, sleeping a certain way to accommodate a sprawling lover. By this point in a relationship we've made fundamental changes in our lives to make the person we love happy. A love affair that ends now, just as a happy future seems in sight, wrenches the heart more violently than it would have a century ago, when the lovers hadn't so much as spent the night together.

How cruel it is, then, that we allow ourselves to come this far in love with no provision for the possibility of an unhappy ending. The reason, I think, is this: Even after coming this far, many of us still don't know if we can commit ourselves to a common future or not. Like timid swimmers creeping to the edge of the high diving board, we try to calm our nerves and imagine ourselves jumping, that is married to or living with this person. And we can't. We didn't decide anything with the first avowal of love, the point at which our ancestors would have struggled to come up with their decision, and we haven't really, finally, decided anything since. Few of us have learned to think ahead when it comes to love. And close as we may get to the moment of truth, to actually jumping, we still desperately want more information, that extra bit of knowledge that will help us take the final step with certainty, or that will release us, at last, from this love.

You'll know when your relationship reaches the "now or never" point, the point at which the future can't be postponed much longer. It's the "now that I've lost everything to you" time that Cat Stevens sings about, when you'll have to decide whether to make a go of it, or not. There's no way around it; not to decide, as the saying goes, is also a way of deciding. It doesn't really matter which of you feels the pull of the future first: Once the urgency to decide is there, it affects you both. Suddenly the future is a palpable presence in the room with you. You bump your head or stub your toe on it every time you move. Unlike most other problems, which simply drift away if you wait around long enough, this one won't disappear until you actually do something about it.

This is an intense time between lovers. You feel the combined forces of love, hope, despair and even mistrust, and there are last-minute longings and accusations in the air. Each of you is looking to the other for some kind of final answer, knowing perfectly well that the answer can come only from within. Until you reach an agreement about the future, until you actually *do* something about it, you have to be very careful of everything you say. When nerves are raw it's much easier to hurt or to be hurt yourself. During this last stage of courtship, when you're frenetically running through your private emotional checklist, it's all too easy to forget about being kind. Your mind is on "what *I* want" and "what *I* need," but as you pull the petals off the daisy this final time, as you come to terms with your love, it's more important than ever to be gentle with your friend, if only because there's more at stake. It's true, you both feel weighted down by all the heavy thinking about the future. Even so, you'll both feel less lonely while making your respective decisions if you take time out from thinking about yourself long enough to remember that this person with whom you fell in love is grappling with the same life-changing decisions you are. Or as a book called *From Marriage to Love* published in the 1930s advised:

Even though love is not a matter of tactics and passion is not an art, affection not a technique, nevertheless he whom the genius of love does not inspire must know the rules of the game, must be clever enough not to give stupid answers to the many questions which the companionship of the sexes put to him. He must have learned the rules.

A few years ago a close friend of mine turned twenty-eight and somehow felt all the anxieties most of us manage to put off until the thirtieth birthday. "My life is going nowhere, what am I going to do with myself, my personal life's a mess, I have no career," blah, blah, blah, she said. "Well, don't think of where you are now," I told her, rather pleased (if I may say so) with this sensible if useless advice. "What do you want to be like when you're thirty?" "I want to be thin," she said, "and married."

It's impossible, at the beginning of a love affair, to think clearly ahead to thirty, forty or fifty, or even to think clearly of what might happen the following week. Part of the unadulterated bliss of a new love affair is that you don't *have* to think. Instead of thinking, "Gee, this probably isn't a good idea because (fill in your own reasons)," you're simply feeling. As a matter of fact, you're feeling fine. You're feeling something like, "If only I could feel this happy all the time I'd never ask for anything else." And because you *are* feeling "this happy" you do forget for the moment about asking for anything else.

What happens, of course, is that after you settle into love, all the things that at first you blithely proclaimed "didn't matter" begin to matter, a lot.

Remember the first night, when you had champagne and tasted escargots for the first time? And he said that he'd had a vasectomy after he and his ex-wife had had the three kids? And you thought, how terrific, I don't have to wear my diaphragm? And making love that night was so great, you felt so free? You remember now, vaguely, that at the time you recalled having read an article about vasectomy reversals, and you (you were only twenty-four at the time, hadn't really begun to think much about children) thought, if it comes to that he can always have it reversed. It didn't seem very important then. But you're twenty-eight now, and now you want children. And he's saying, "But you knew all along about the vasectomy. You knew I didn't want any more children."

Or, at the beginning, remember how impressed you were that she was an actress? She wasn't a very successful actress, of course, she'd only appeared in a few things off-Broadway. To earn her living what she really did was to work as an office temp. What you admired, really, was that unwavering belief she had in herself, her certainty that she would one day make it. That was two years ago, and now it turns out she was right: She's on the verge of making it. When she flew out to Hollywood for two weeks last spring to make the pilot you didn't think much about it. She'd had parts that almost worked out before. But the show has financing now; it's been accepted by a network. And you've seen it—it's good. To do the show she'll have to move out to the Coast, at least for a year, maybe longer. She wants you to move with her, give up your whole life here. "We talked about it all along," she says. "I told you that when everything worked out I'd probably have to move."

Or, you remember how at the beginning you thought it was kind of sweet when he had a little too much to drink; he got so sentimental. But now you wonder whether his drinking might turn into a problem.... At first, when she'd talk about how much she wanted a baby you thought that yes, maybe that could work out. But now she's not talking about having a baby someday. She's talking about having one *soon*, like in about nine months. And now you're not so sure about the whole thing, the screaming, the diapers.... You both agreed when you met that marriage was out of the question; both your marriages had been disastrous. It was such a relief, that kind of relationship, no hassles. But now he's beginning to think that you should get married, give it another try. And you're not sure at all that that's what you want to do.... You and she used to make jokes about it, her dream to move to the country once you decided to settle down. I mean, it never really seemed like an *issue*. Now that you've discussed getting married, however, all she talks about is how much she despises the city, how filthy and uncivilized it is. You think the city is just fine. And for some reason you had assumed that the question of where you'd live was negotiable.

Once push comes to shove in a romance, all the who-you-are, what-you-want, where-you're-going questions that used to be academic suddenly become real. Instead of saying, "Of course, my darling, anything you want," you find yourself saying, "Wait a minute. Stop. We can't do that. No, I *never* promised. What do you think I am, a millionaire? I hate canopy beds. No, I don't want to go into your family's business. And how can you think of buying a video recorder when what we'll really need is a kitchen table?" You feel as if the person you fell in love with has disappeared and has been replaced by this new monster, who is demanding from you things that you were never prepared to give, or refusing you what you knew all along you needed. You feel almost as if you've been deceived while you, of course, have been the same person all along.

But you haven't been the same person all along, either, and the truth is that you appear to your friend as much of a monster as he or she appears to you.

What happens at this point in a love affair is much like what happened to the kids who grew up in the Sixties.

In their jeans, fringed suede vests and granny glasses these "hippies" hung around stoned for a while, living a fantasy and having a wonderful time, and then sooner or later most of them went back to real life, replacing their whimsical costumes with the suits required for getting on in the real world. The jeans now are allowed out only on weekends. Similarly, the fantasy of a new love must sooner or later give in to the real concerns of living day to day. The spirit of love remains with you all the time, just as the children of the Sixties will always dream about a better world, but the perfect love you saw at the beginning will, under the demands of an imperfect world, fray a little around the edges. Cynical as this may sound, what we all try to do is to make our peace with love as it is, and hope for a glimpse of the real thing on weekends.

And it's only now that you're finding out what your love is really like. There's a lot to digest, now that the moats and turrets you've dreamed of all your life have come down to whether or not you can afford a condo with a one-car garage. You've imagined a couple of adorable little children romping in a garden wearing white play clothes, and now you remember that you and your lover are nearsighted and tend to gain weight. Will your kids be fat and myopic? Then out of the blue your lover says, "I think we should have at least six kids," and suddenly you see a herd of fat, nearsighted little children running around the condo. You go out happily one Saturday morning to look at furniture, after a romantic Friday night of planning your lives together, vowing that you'll never prepare dinner from ingredients that have to be defrosted, and your lover makes a beeline for the ugliest end table you've ever seen and says, "This would be divine next to the wing chair my mother promised me when I got married." You've seen the wing chair, you hate the table and your heart sinks.

Put that phone down. You can't escape by calling up for a seat on the next flight to Singapore. Wing chairs always come as a shock at first; many times they'll come to grow on you. Stay calm. The impulse to flee from love at the first sign of reality lies within all of us. Did it ever occur to you that your lover might feel about your mahogany eagle the way you do about the wing chair? Listen to what your lover has to say about the future, and say what you have to say, too. You can't begin to make compromises until all the factors that might have to be compromised are out in the open. Your first pimple will tell you that your childhood is over; your first phone bill will tell you you're no longer a carefree adolescent. You may contemplate suicide at the sight of your first wrinkle. And your first Wing Chair Incident will give you a clue that there's more to love than champagne and candlelight.

Unfairly enough, even as you're facing up bravely to the big issues, this is a time when you'll also have to face up to the little things of love. For example, it's easy to forget how noble a character your boyfriend, Ranger, really is when you want to kick him every morning because he never remembers to fold the towels and put them back on the rack, but lets them fall to the bathroom floor instead. You're not even living together officially yet, and it still drives you crazy. You've noticed that his mother and father know all about towel-folding, and there doesn't seem to be a problem with this at his sister's house—and she's got all those kids and a husband who drinks beer in his T-shirt, which Ranger would never think of doing. You've said gently, "Range, I'd really love it if you would learn to fold the towels and put them back on the rack where they belong." Every time you go through this routine he looks contrite, apologizes, agrees you're right, promises to try harder in the future. He never does. And while you're at it, why does he have to cross his heart every time he promises anything?

In love, it's the little things, the nasty little mannerisms that always seemed so touching the first time you noticed them, that make the big things seem insignificant. You used to gaze with delight at her dainty things hanging in the bathroom, remember? You used to feel so close to her when you saw the leotard she wears to weight-lifting classes draped over the shower-curtain rod. You could reach out and touch it if you wanted. But now you notice that she leaves it there whenever she's not in fact lifting weights. You really wish she'd learn to put it away between classes.

I once had dinner with a woman long divorced who began confiding in me the pros and cons of marriage. The cons didn't seem so bad, and finally I asked her the real reason she and her husband had broken up. "Real reason? I'm not sure. What I always think of is that he used to put the toilet paper on so that you had to pull it out from under. I was taught that the right way is for the paper to come over the top. We used to fight about that, and by the end we were always switching the toilet paper around on each other. When you get to that point it's time to get out."

There is no way to avoid the possibility that one day you'll be driven mad because your dearest one says "you know" before every sentence, or because he or she *always* leaves drinking glasses in the kitchen sink without ever rinsing them off. For every irritating habit you manage to overlook there's always another one lurking right behind. On the questionnaires, I asked the respondents to list specific irritations that had come up in their serious relationships. Here are some of them, along with a few rules to remember in dealing with the inevitable annoyances that are bound to accompany someone with whom you might come to share your life:

1. The overwhelming number of complaints have to do with bathroom etiquette. If you are doing any of the following you can be sure you're getting on someone's nerves, or that you will be: leaving rings around the tub or hair in the sink; violating toothpaste tubes in any way or losing the caps; the already cited towel-folding and clothes-hanging-to-dry habits; gracing the floor with your footprints; forgetting to wipe off steamy mirrors. Gentlemen: toilet seats should always be left down, because I said so. Ladies: bottles and jars should always be put away after use, unless you're really in a hurry.

2. If you're contemplating a life together or even if you're not, it is none of your business how your other half keeps his or her private quarters. Private quarters include drawers, closets (don't get involved with anyone unless you can be sure of eventual separate closets), pocketbooks, desks, floors of closets, toolsheds and darkrooms.

3. Many complaints also arise from breaking the rules of bedroom etiquette. Avoid leaving your clothes on the floor, bed, lamps or backs of chairs, unless your partner does too. Leave only as much of your stuff (e.g., cosmetics, hairdriers, magazines, hobby and athletic equipment, experiments, papers and accessories) lying around as the other party does. The equal-mess theory will help stabilize any long-term arrangement, and should be practiced beginning now in every room of the house.

4. People who don't smoke, bite their nails, twist their hair, cough, sneeze or blow their noses a lot, wear rumpled clothing, chew gum, fidget with eyeglasses, play with their toes or hum are often annoyed by those who do.

Among those who practice these or related habits, they are as important to the quality of life as breathing. Make your defensive adjustments: If your friend hums, for example, try loud singing.

5. People who are always on time invariably come to blows with people who are always late. Conversely, people who are always late are usually impatient if they're told to hurry. If you and your lover have this problem, don't get married.

6. Never eat ice cream right from the container with a spoon or the peanut butter directly from the jar with your finger, unless you are absolutely certain that your friend is in Seattle (and you're not). And never leave kitchen mini-messes to be cleaned up by good fairies. There are no such good fairies.

7. Male chauvinism is unacceptable, as are displays of helplessness because one is a woman (unless you're facing a mouse). Before you say "could you get me?" or "would you mind?" ask yourself whether you could get it just as easily, or whether you know ahead of time that he or she would definitely mind.

8. It is important to cultivate the appearance of listening for those times when you're not listening at all. When you're reminded later that, "I *told* you about the dent," you must make yourself say, "Yes, you did. I remember now."

9. Of course you could tell the story better and you wouldn't leave out all the good parts, either. But the story belongs to the person who gets to it first.

10. A man I once met reflected sadly, "I don't know what it is, but doesn't it seem that we don't try as hard with the people we love?" "Please" and "thank you," those endangered words, never lose their charm. Men and women never outgrow their basic human need to be complimented. A good rule of thumb is to be as polite

to the people you love as you would be to a tax auditor. The tricky thing about manners and love is that there will always be times when, no matter how much in love you are, you can't summon up your responses from the heart. That's when simple common courtesy is most important.

In a short story by Joy Williams called "Breakfast," the character Charlie, musing about love, observes that, "There are not as many ways of making love as people seem to believe." In the privacy of your dreams, it's easy to imagine endless possibilities for love. But when you're awake it's much harder to accept life's limitations. It's the heart that tells you about the possibilities—and the mind that fills you in on the odds. Throughout the early stages of courtship you've been acting on the impulses of the heart. It's time now to reconcile what your heart has told you with all that your mind has to say.

"Tracy and Egon are going to live together! I can't believe it. She's so, I don't know, *serious*, and he's so—um—flamboyant. Like showing up at that party at Mr. Scrudge's house that time with the squirt gun."

Curious as other people's affairs are to outsiders, only the people involved can tell if the thing "makes sense." And the thing has got to make sense, has got to have an internal logic, if what you're aiming for is a happily-ever-after ending. Only you can ascertain whether there's a logic beyond outward appearances to your relationship, the kind of logic that will keep your love running, and that's both solid and flexible enough to sustain you both in the years to come. And as much in touch with your feelings as you think you are, there's more to long-term love than good sex and a shared preference for double cheese and pepperoni on your pizza. It's well-advised, then, to spend some time analyzing rationally just how deep this love of yours goes.

In many ways ours is a remarkably unstructured society. We can live our adult lives without paying much attention to the religious, social or economic dictates of our early years. In fact, most of us are virtually expected to "create" a life of our own once we reach adulthood. When it comes to falling in love, we think first of what we're like here and now, forgetting for a time how it is that we got there: If you're going through a bohemian phase you'll fall in love with a bohemian. We rarely stop to ask the questions that would have been our ancestors' first considerations, the questions of plausibility. What religion are you? Are you a Democrat? How do you plan to spend your retirement? Do you like Danish modern furniture? Would you like your kids to go to Montessori schools?

But we're talking real life now, not hearts and flowers, and you're not as simple a creature as the person you were when you fell in love. You're also full of ideas you learned a long time ago about how life should be conducted, and it's a good idea to compare with your lover the traditions under which you both grew up, to make sure that there's some foundation there to hold you together once you move on to being the person you'll become next. Tradition dies hard in us, and crops up in unexpected ways. You'd be amazed at how many after-the-fact fights erupt because *her* mother always had cornbread stuffing with the Thanksgiving turkey and *his* always stuffed the damn thing with oysters.

The future won't just happen. You have to plan for it, hope for it, control it insofar as you can and decide what can be decided ahead of time. You're not ready for the future yet if you can't sit down together and talk seriously about such things as what family traditions you'd like to maintain; where and how you'd like to live (*not* in a "wouldn't it be nice to buy San Simeon?" way); whether there are to be children and when, and how you'd raise them; basic things like whether one of you would happily blow your life savings on a lavish vacation while the other would prefer to spend the money on matching avocado-colored kitchen appliances; and anything else you can think of that matters to you. When you first set up house together is generally not the best time for surprises.

Another consideration is to figure out ahead of time what role your "living past" and your lover's will play in your future. Our ancestors, who usually married once and at an early age, never had to worry about things like whether for the child's sake it wouldn't be right to include the ex-husband at little Katie's birthday party. But many of us, with our unorthodox ties and complicated histories, find that the past is like quicksand and there's no way, even if we wanted to, to get out of it.

"I can't help it. I get really jealous," a young woman told me, describing her boy friend's relationship with his ex-girl friend. "He sees her all the time and they talk practically every day. I know he wouldn't go back to her, but they're really close. I have this feeling that they talk about things he doesn't talk about with me."

Many of us have such "ghosts" from our pasts that may be hard for the newcomer to take. And our ghosts are more numerous and confusing than the ghosts that haunted earlier generations. It's complicated to hate an ex-girl friend. There's no category in which to put her. People expect you to complain about an ex-spouse, for example—that's perfectly normal. But an *ex-girl friend*? When there's no chance they'll get back together again? So what's the big problem? So what if they're friends? Yet you still hate her.

Or how do you say to someone, "I'd love to marry you but I can't stand your kid?" You can joke publicly about a difficult mother-in-law, but what have we got ourselves into these days when we have to make room in our feelings for all sorts of people we never invited into our lives?

It's painful to acknowledge that someone you love has loved others before, has seen happiness without you and that the memories of this past happiness are still living, breathing, calling on the phone. (Was the other happiness better? Did you love him more than you love me? What was the sex like? Was she funny, funnier than me?)

On the other hand, you too have a right to your ghosts, along with the right to be happy now, in a new love, a new life. But just as a new table is made of an old tree, a new life bears the influences, good and bad, of all that went on before. There's no such thing as a brand-new life.

There are anthropologists who argue that jealousy turns up only in "finely developed" cultures like ours. Big deal. Anyway, that's not very consoling, unless you're planning to move to the jungles of Inner Scherbia. Most of us understand jealousy very well: When you freeze in place in utter hatred, mortification and self-righteousness, force an expression of detachment and mild distaste, and hope that the person you love most in the world will choke when there's nobody around to perform the Heimlich maneuver, that's jealousy.

Sexual jealousy, where you know absolutely in your bones for certain that maybe your lover is probably flirting with the lady in red or the gentleman in green (*green?*) is an emotion which most of us know too well. But we also know that we have certain rights when we sense a sexual threat: we are behaving correctly to yell, throw a tantrum, drag our lover away and create as unpleasant a scene as possible. Public sympathy is with us. But the vague uneasiness that comes with other kinds of jealousy—the sense that what with the ex-husband or wife, the kids, the former lovers, the high-pressure job, the demanding friends who seem to be around all the time, there won't be room for *me*, for the kind of life that I want—is a different matter. You can hold your own, you feel, with a sexual rival, but how can you hold your own with a life that's already filled up, whether you're there or not?

Reconciling the past with the present can be the most difficult negotiation in working out a permanent relationship. "Yes, let's live together, but only if you put away the wedding picture from your first marriage where you and George are cutting the wedding cake." "Okay, I'll marry you, but not unless I can ride in the front seat from now on when your kids come to visit." "All right, we'll get a place together but first you have to promise that you will never again mention how it ruined your life when your first girlfriend, Kitty, moved to Chicago when you were six." Standing up for your rights in these cases puts you in the unenviable position of scotching someone's cherished memories and obsessions.

Only when you've taken everything into account that can be taken into account can you judge the compromises you are willing to make—and those you are not.

It's scary, putting yourself on the line by saying, "Unless you can do this, I can't do that," but that's the only way you'll ever know if your love is spacious enough to encompass you both.

In the Code of Hammurabi, the set of ancient Babylonian laws that in one form or another survived as the basis for many later legal systems, there are two hundred fifty-two laws. Of these, 64, one quarter, were rules for marriage. Not who-walks-the-dog or who-empties-the-garbage kinds of rules, but rules that set marriage up as the central institution that holds the culture together and keeps it orderly. In the long run Babylon didn't make it, but marriage did. To contemplate marriage from the point of view of the song that says "all you need is love" is to fail to see what Hammurabi saw: that love brings with it rules and conditions and for-better-or-for-worse responsibilities. To ignore all the ifs and buts that concerned the ancients is to risk ending up in a divorce lawyer's office a few years hence, feeling like a lonely and confused child who doesn't know whether he abandoned the world or the world deserted him. Marriage is called a solemn institution because the decision to marry or even to live together requires you to come to terms not only with your love, but with every bit of will and strength and self-knowledge you possess.

And even after all this, sometimes it still doesn't work.

A few months ago I ran into a friend who had recently stopped seeing a man she had gone out with, semi-lived with, for nearly three years. I asked her how she was doing. "Better," she said, but then in an almost apologetic tone she added, "I only started going out again a couple of weeks ago." But why did she *apologize* for spending a few months privately grieving for someone she had loved so much? Why can't we see that a love that ultimately fails must once have been a love that worked? Doesn't a love that ends still count as a legitimate love?

The saddest endings are those where the lovers come all this way before one bewildered lover turns to the other and says: "It won't work." But why? The love is there, the memories, the shared friends, the secret jokes, two promising futures. Why? "I don't know, I can't explain it. Maybe we just want different things." But why? What did I do wrong? The saddest endings come when the person who leaves is as sad as the person left behind.

It's not very satisfying to lay down "rules" for breaking up because it's impossible to legislate decency: Either it's there or it's not. I think that the man who sleeps with a woman owes her at least an "I'm glad we did this; it meant something to me. But maybe I shouldn't have slept with you: In all honesty I don't want to be involved right now." Past that stage, a lover deserves the truth, presented as simply and as gracefully as possible. If the reason is another love, a breakdown in trust or the loss of feelings, the person who is to be left has a right to know. It takes time, but in most cases it's easier, with time, to deal with the truth. A lover also deserves to be told at the right moment—not that there is ever exactly the right moment, but some moments are better than others. One man I talked to, for example, was bitter because his lover had left him on the night after his son had had a major operation. "Can you believe it? She told me that night at dinner. I'd been through so much that day." The other side of that coin, however, is that his lover—who obviously had decided some time earlier that she was leaving—waited to break up with him so that she could be with him during the operation.

What are unacceptable are the deliberately cruel methods of breaking up. I read in a magazine once about the "Dump a Date" service, an organization with an "800" number to call that, for a nominal sum, will take care of the nasty matter for you. More recently I read about a line of "greeting" cards with varying "see you around" messages to choose from; the cards apparently are selling very well. I can't imagine anything more cruel than having a lover say goodbye to me through the mail.

Cowardice in breaking up is only slightly better than

deliberate cruelty. A woman I know, for example, began a relationship that had thrived for about a year even though the two lived in different cities. They had talked about living together once his divorce was final; she was willing to move to be with him. But he cancelled one of the weekends they had planned. Then he stopped calling. No one answered his home phone. And when my friend called his office she was always told that he was "in a meeting." Finally she asked a friend to call his office and claim to be another friend of his. She took over the phone when he picked it up—and confronted him. This dishonorable coward had gone back to his wife. Poor wife.

I refuse to believe that any of us enters a relationship with the idea in mind: "I'm going to fall in love with this person, then we're going to spend a lot of time together, then we're going to talk about making a go of it and *then* I'm going to break his or her heart. Won't that be fun?"

What happens instead is that we start out in all innocence and hope, postpone the thinking and the choices in favor of the happiness for as long as we can, then come to see what we either knew all along or didn't. And when one of us, crying, says, "It just won't work," that's about all there is to say. The logic, the rationale, isn't there to balance out the love. To the question, "What did I do wrong?" the only truthful answer is, "Nothing. You did nothing wrong."

Ours is perhaps not the most efficient way to arrange for the orderly progression of new generations, but it's all we've got at the moment. And the most we can ask from each other is that we pursue courtship and love with honorable intentions, that we say where we stand the minute we know where we stand. A book called *Hints for Lovers* published more than seventy years ago says that, "A man imagines he wins by strenuous assault. The woman knows the victory was due to surrender." In fact, there's rarely a *victor* in love; love instead is a matter of something there to begin with, more hard work than you ever bargained for, strength and generosity of spirit—and a measure of luck.

Ten, nine, eight, seven, six, five....

It's amazing to think that all systems could possibly be go in a spaceship, that it could actually get off the ground. You'd think that at the last minute the astronaut would stop the countdown when he remembered that he had forgotten the only pillow he can sleep with, or his vitamins.

It's even more amazing to think that, with all that could go wrong, all systems can be go in a love affair: that you'll reach a point where without qualification you can say, "Yeah, okay. A life with you is what I want."

On my questionnaires I asked, "Does courtship lead to marriage?" The question seems pointless until you remember that courtship was once the express lane to marriage—now we're less sure about it. For us courtship more often than not doesn't lead to marriage. So instead of a resounding, "Yes, of course," the answers to this question were, "Maybe," "It could," "It's supposed to," "Yes, but no" or "No, but yes." As I read these replies I could almost hear the embarrassed mumbling.

Well, courtship does lead to marriage (that or living together which itself usually leads to marriage, especially with the housing shortage the way it is), or it might and, yes, it's supposed to.

Not that you'll get married, lean back in your wing chair, relax and say, "Phew." That won't happen either; marriage is just as difficult and confusing as courtship, a variation on the same theme. As Theodore Dreiser wrote in *Sister Carrie*, "Courtship is the text from which the whole sermon of married life takes its theme." The difference, I suppose, is that you can't storm out and go home (you *are* home), and you'll never again have the satisfaction of calling up in the middle of the night to wake your lover from a sound sleep by saying, "And *furthermore!*" But there must be compensations.

As for embracing the future without qualification, I don't think it's possible. With something as final as a marriage license there will always be doubts. Some people have last-minute flings or last-minute cold feet. A friend of mine who was about to be married called the marriage bureau in New York and reached a recording, which in a monotone started to tell her about blood tests, license requirements, fees. She slammed down the phone in the middle of the recording and said, "I can't go through with this." But then she dialed the number again, listened to the recording all the way through, and now she's married. In the Soviet Union, a couple, upon obtaining a marriage license, is required to wait a month before they marry. During the wait, 12 percent of Soviet relationships fall apart. On the other hand, 88 percent don't.

One of the mysteries of love is that not all people love in the same way. You can't say this is love, or this isn't, and in fact some people will always be better at loving, more patient with it, than others. But it's heartening to see a symbiosis between two people, where one knows without question that even if the other's behavior seems a little weird to that casual observer, that's just his or her way of "showing love." "That means he loves me," or, "That's just her way."

And the other mystery is that love, no matter how good you are at it or how much you know about it, will always remain a mystery. To say "yes" to love is to give yourself wholeheartedly to a feeling, a hope, you'll never fully understand. The poet John Keats knew this, knew that sometimes we have to feel our way around by following the instincts that make us human, and he called it Negative Capability:

That is when man is capable of being in uncertainties, Mysteries, doubts, without any irritable reaching after fact and reason....

Selected Bibliography

The following books were particularly helpful to me; many, in addition, are enormous fun to read.

Alcott, William A., M.D. *Moral Philosophy of Courtship and Marriage*. Boston: John P. Jewett & Co., 1857.

Archbald, Anna. *The Fusser's Book: Rules by Anna Archbald*. New York: Fox, Duffield Co., 1904.

Aresty, Esther B. *The Best Behavior: The Course of Good Manners—From Antiquity to the Present—As Seen Through Courtesy & Etiquette Books*. New York: Simon & Schuster, 1962.

Baldridge, Letitia (Revised & Expanded by). *The Amy Vanderbilt Complete Book of Etiquette*. Garden City, New York: Doubleday, 1978.

Basch, Rudolph. *How Did It Begin? Customs & Supersititions, and Their Romantic Origins*. New York: David McKay Co., 1966.

Bell, Lilian. *Why Men Remain Bachelors & Other Luxuries*. New York: John Lane Co., The Bodley Head, 1906.

Brooks, John. *Showing Off in America: From Conspicuous Consumption to Parody Display*. Boston: Atlantic-Little, Brown, 1981.

Brown, Helen Gurley. *Sex and the Single Girl*. New York: Pocket Books, 1963.

Bulfinch, Thomas. *The Age of Chivalry*. New York: Airmont Publishing Company, 1965.

Calverton, V. F. and S. D. Schmaulhausen. *Sex in Civilization*, Introduction by Havelock Ellis. New York: The Macauley Co., 1929.

de Ropp, Robert S. *Sex Energy: The Sexual Force in Man and Animals*. New York: A Seymour Lawrence Book / Delcorte, 1969.

de Rougement, Denis. *Love in the Western World*. Translated by Montgomery Belgion. New York: Harper Torchbooks, 1974.

D'Orsay, Count Alfred. *Etiquette, or a Guide to the Usages of Society with a Glance at Bad Habits*. New York: Wilson & Co., 1843.

Eichler, Lillian. *The Customs of Mankind With Notes on Modern Etiquette and The Newest Trend in Entertainment*. Garden City, New York: Doubleday, 1924.

Ellis, Havelock. *Psychology of Sex: A Manual for Students*. New York: Ray Long and Richard R. Smith, Inc., 1933.

Emerson, Ralph Waldo. *Essays*. New York: Crowell, Apollo Ed., 1961.

Fielding, William J. *Strange Customs of Courtship and Marriage*. Garden City, New York: Garden City Books/Doublday, 1960.

Goffman, Ervin. *The Presentation of Self in Everyday Life*. New York: Anchor Books, 1959.

Grand, Sara. *The Modern Man and Maid*. London: Horace Marshall & Son, 1898.

Harbin, E. O. *Phunology: A Collection of Tried and Proved Plans for Play, Fellowship, and Profit*. Nashville, Tennessee: Cokesbury Press, 1923.

Harland, Marion, and Virginia Van de Water. *Everyday Etiquette: A Practical Manual of Social Usages*. Indianapolis: Bobbs-Merrill, 1907.

Haultain, Arnold. *Hints for Lovers*. New York: Houghton Mifflin, 1909.

Hopton, Dr. Ralph Y., and Anne Balliol. *Bed Manners and Better Bed Manners: How To Bring Sunshine Into Your Nights*. New York: Arden Book Co., 1948.

Hunt, Morton. *Sexual Behavior in the 1970s*. New York: Playboy Press, 1974.

Johns, Jane. *The Girls Men Marry*. New York: E. P. Dutton, 1929.

Kerouac, Jack. *On the Road*. New York: Signet Books (NAL), 1957.

Lebowitz, Fran. *Social Studies*. New York: Random House, 1981.

Lewinsohn, Richard. *A History of Sexual Customs*. Translated by Alexander Mayce. New York: Harper & Bros., 1958.

Lewis, C. S. *The Allegory of Love: A Study in Medieval Tradition*. London: Oxford University Press, 1976.

Loebel, Josep, M.D. *From Marriage to Love*. New York: Ives Washburn, 1930.

McCullough, David. *Mornings on Horseback*. New York: Simon & Schuster, 1981.

Moore, Mrs. Clara Sophia Jessup. *Sensible Etiquette of the Best Society*. 18th revised edition. Philadelphia: Porter & Coates, 1878.

Norbert, Elias. *The Civilizing Process: The History of Manners*. New York: Horizon Press, 1978.

Nyrop, Dr. Christopher. *The Kiss and Its History*. New York: E. P. Dutton, 1902.

Putnam, Emily James. *The Lady: Studies of Certain Significant Phases of Her History*. Chicago: University of Chicago Press, 1970.

Reik, Theodore. *Of Love and Lust*. New York: Pyramid Books, 1976.

Rofes, Eric E., ed. *The Kids' Book of Divorce, By, For and About Kids, By the Unit at Fayerweather Street School*. Lexington, Massachusetts: The Lewis Publishing Co., 1981.

Russell, Bertrand. *Marriage and Morals*. New York: Liveright, 1970.

Severn, Bill. *The Long and Short of It: Five Thousand Years of Fun and Fury Over Hair*. New York: David McKay, 1971.

Stendhal. *Love*. Translated by Gilbert and Suzanne Sale. New York: Penguin Books, 1980.

Stiles, Henry Reed. *Bundling: Its Origin, Progress and Decline in America*. Privately Issued, Reprinted from Edition of 1871.

Szasz, Thomas. *Sex by Prescription*. New York: Anchor Press/Doubleday, 1980.

Turner, E. S. *A History of Courting*. New York: E. P. Dutton, 1955.

Vanderbilt, Amy. *Etiquette*. Garden City, New York: Doubleday, 1972.

Vanderbilt, Amy. *Everyday Etiquette: Answers to Today's Etiquette Questions*. Second Revised Edition. New York: Bantam, 1974.

Vatsyayana. *Kama Sutra: The Hindu Ritual of Love*. New York: Castle Books, 1968.

Wallace, Lily Haxworth, ed. *The New American Etiquette*. New York: Books, Inc., 1947.

Ward, Mrs. H. O. (pseudonym for Clara S. J. Moore). *Young Lady's Friend*. Philadelphia: Porter & Coates, 1880.

Webster's Ready-Made Love Letters. New York: Robert M. De Witt, 1873.

Wurdz, Gideon. *Eediotic Etiquette*. Cambridge, Massachusetts: The University Press, Frederick Stokes & Co., 1906.

Index

CHERYL MERSER lives in New York, where she works for a major publisher. This is her first book.